"Patricia Williams has written *ONCE UPON A LIFETIME...* Thank goodness. It is indeed a once in a lifetime book, full of the most beautiful and enjoyable ways to take a good look at your life, the life of your best friend, wife, husband, father, mother, grandmother, grandfather, son, daughter, or anyone else of importance to you. Taking a good look means taking a positive and noble look at life, seeing the best of your successes and failures, recording all your achievements, goals, dreams, and wishes. To see where one goal has led to another, different, better, more refined achievement. What emerges is a sense of pride and strength, of peaceful calm, of the humble knowledge of intimacy. Use *ONCE UPON A LIFETIME...* as a personal diary, journal, observation, and skill exercise book... a companion on your journey.

For me, *ONCE UPON A LIFETIME...* has been three gifts in one. In my practice, it serves as a sensitive and practical way to remind people about the positive parts of their life they might otherwise have forgotten, leading to greater insight and a higher level of personal satisfaction. The other two parts of her gift have been in my own life. In one, her book works the same magic of closeness, connection, and sense of belonging, to myself and to my family. The other is the most awesome and magnificent part of her gift, of meeting Patricia Williams, who has become my friend. Thank you, Patri̇ı̇ "

David P̲

"One of the most important t̲ ̲ ̲ ̲o value is your family. Knowing their history adds a significant dimension to your own life. Everyone should have Patricia's special book that makes it so easy to record past and present events. Turn the pages and learn more about yourself while sharing your thoughts and experiences. Generations to come will treasure these memories."

Jean Paré
Author, *Company's Coming* cookbooks

"Patricia Williams has an exquisite understanding of the power and importance of our individual and family stories. She has crafted here an impressive array of questions to ignite the imagination and tease up quiet details and subtle nuances of our life stories. *ONCE UPON A LIFETIME...* enables us to mine precious gems which might otherwise lie forgotten. Reconnecting in this intentional way with events, people, and memories of our past reconnects us in some essential way with our deepest selves; hence not only is this book a precious gift for younger generations of our families, but it is an empowering journey for each of us who writes in these pages."

Marcy Wineman Axness
Adoption Educator
Calabasas, CA

"What a great relationship building book! I use *ONCE UPON A LIFETIME...* as a valuable gift to my clients. As their trusted financial advisor, their families are also important to me. If I give them a book that can help them leave a legacy of memories to their loved ones, I have given them a gift more valuable than financial gifts."

Bryan Godtland
Investment Centers of America
Hudson, WI

"I gave a copy of *ONCE UPON A LIFETIME...* to my mother for Christmas this year - what a gift it has been! Questions in your book have triggered emotions in my mother that for years she has never expressed. It has inspired my mother to attempt contacting a son whom she put up for adoption over 41 years ago! *ONCE UPON A LIFETIME...* has enabled us to open up the communication lines - we have sat around for hours sharing memories of her past. Thank you for producing such a treasure!!"

Sara Dewald
Edmonton, Alberta

"Patricia Williams has given us a magnificent guide for the stories, the wisdom, the visions, and the love from precious moments in our lives for our children to have and cherish. A gift that will endear itself to those whom we love and many generations to come."

Woodie M. Montgomery, RFC, CEC
Montgomery Planning Services, Inc.
Atlanta, GA

"Teach us to number our days that we may gain a heart of wisdom."
Psalm 90:12

"Family memories and traditions are the threads that weave generations together. How wonderful it is to recall special times with special people in our lives. *ONCE UPON A LIFETIME...* facilitates with great ease our recalling and recording the specific and unique aspects of our life and times. As you work through its pages, *ONCE UPON A LIFETIME...* takes the colorful threads of your life and weaves your unique history to pass to the next generation... a treasure that only you could provide to your family."

Larry W. Carroll, CFP, CMFC
Carroll Financial Associates
Charlotte, NC

"We are very pleased with the response to our client Christmas gifts of your book *ONCE UPON A LIFETIME...* Our cover letter indicated we wanted our clients and their families to enjoy remembering special people, places and times in their lives as they gathered for the holidays. The comments we received indicated that they did indeed receive great pleasure from sharing your book with both young and older family members alike, and working on a legacy for the entire family to have for generations to come. Your book is certainly a timeless gift!"

Dinverno & Foltz Financial Group
Oak Brook, IL

"I bought the book *ONCE UPON A LIFETIME...* for my father last Christmas. He balked at the idea of filling out a bunch of questions about his life. I hounded him to do it for a few months.

He said he'd done the first page in January, and the second page in February, but was having a hard time getting into it. He isn't one to talk about himself or his life, but I knew he'd had a very adventurous and challenging life, and I had always wanted to know more about it. He'd never shown us any photo albums, has no family, and wanted to "leave the past behind." I stopped bugging him about the book a few months ago. Three weeks ago he died in his home of a sudden heart attack. He was 81 years old. As my sister and I were going through his things, on his desk, under a big pile of books and papers was the book of questions *ONCE UPON A LIFETIME...*

I noticed that he had not only filled in the first two pages, but every page of the book. He had answered all 1001 questions. If not with an answer, at least with "N.A."

I told the story of the book at his memorial service and quoted from it. People told me how moving it was to hear about his life, and have quotes from the book. I've had a least 15 people ask me where to get a copy of the book so they can give it to their parents. Thank you very much - it's an amazing book!"

Carla Rieger
Vancouver, B.C.

Once Upon a Lifetime...

Creating a legacy for future generations

Written and compiled by
Patricia A. Williams

Twelfth printing August 2000

ISBN 0-9681400-0-9

Published and distributed by

The Time Broker Inc.
P.O. Box 37066
Edmonton, Alberta, Canada T5R 5Y2

Telephone: 780-486-3248
Fax: 780-486-2380
E-mail: pwilliams@storiesofyourlife.com
Web: www.storiesofyourlife.com

Available in French under title: "Il était une fois... ma vie"
ISBN 2-89249-806-6

PC-Version also available

Printed in Canada by
Nisku Printers (1980) Ltd., Nisku, Alberta

Canadian Cataloguing in Publication Data

Williams, Patricia A., 1941-
    Once upon a lifetime... : creating a legacy for future generations
ISBN 0-9681400-0-9
    1. Autobiography. 2. Biography as a literary form. I. Title
CS16.W53 1996   808'.06692   C96-901021-4

DEDICATION

*To my family and friends
who have given me the power for my dream*

"Climb the mountain and catch a new vision"

CONTENTS

INTRODUCTION

WHERE HAVE YOU STORED YOUR MEMORIES?

*This could be the most important book you'll ever write in,
as it touches on questions of the heart and soul.*

*Your family knows the outer you,
but needs to be connected with the inner you.*

Many people today are searching for knowledge about the past, and especially about the history of their families. Unfortunately, it is usually after the death of a loved one that families realize a wealth of wisdom and history has been lost, and can never be retrieved. Daughters, sons, and grandchildren may be left thinking, "If only someone had taken the time to capture those precious memories before it was too late!"

With our hurried and transient lifestyles, and the distances, divorces, and deaths that may separate us, preserving stories of the past may not be a priority for many of us. Even well-intentioned people may allow years to go by because they don't know where or how to begin to save their memories. But who else can leave a factual account of your past but you?

Once Upon a Lifetime… was designed to help you to write your own life stories or, if you prefer, to use as a guide in recording your stories on audiotape or videotape. You will note that several sections include words such as "did/do" and "was/is." This is because the person you are being asked about may still be living. The easy-to-use format enables you to gather your memories in installments—a step at a time. The task of extracting stories will not seem quite so daunting if you use the questions to help you recall your memories in a logical sequence.

There will, of course, be omissions, since no set of questions could account for the immense variety of human experiences, but in general, this book will provide a comprehensive overview of its author's life.

Once this book has been completed, family can reminisce and tell each other stories as they read through the questions and answers. Their stories can also be documented and added to your book.

Good luck as you embark on this most important adventure. Those people who are privileged to receive a book from you will be thrilled that you have taken the time to care about preserving the past for the future. What better gift can you present your family with but *a gift of time!*

HOW TO USE THIS BOOK

PREPARATION

- Decide if you will record answers to questions in handwriting or if you will be recording responses on audiotape or videotape; then purchase or assemble the tools that you will need.

- Purchase a journal or notebook in which you can write or expand stories from the questions provided. As you answer many of the questions, you will find your memory prompts you to write many other stories. There are five specific sections that will require use of a journal or notebook in order to accommodate writing about all family members (Memories of Grandparents, Memories of Siblings, Memories of Extended Family, Memories of Parenting, and Memories of Grandparenting).

- Gather the documents and personal records you wish to read to stimulate your memory (see Before You Begin section).

- Decide where and when you can spend time on this undertaking. If you decide to work on this project at home, it is a good idea to set aside a specific area where your papers won't be disturbed and where you feel comfortable and stimulated to write.

- Consider purchasing an extra notebook that you can use to record any spontaneous thoughts as they occur, even if they are not related to the category you're working on at the moment. You will want to incorporate this information at a later date. (This notebook will be separate from your final memoir.)

- Make sure you will not be distracted during your reminiscing times.

- Plan to write or record your stories at a specific time each day, or week, for continuity — preferably your peak time of day.

- This book has 1,001 questions. Not all questions will apply to each person. You can answer the questions as they appear or take some time to review them and check off the ones you want to respond to. (There is a box before each question for this purpose.)

- Begin with the section entitled "The Present". It is much easier to recall present-day facts and stories. Once you start reminiscing, you will find the past comes into view much more easily. You may wish to work through the sections in order, or focus first on those segments of your life that hold the most meaning for you.

BEFORE YOU BEGIN

Keeping your memory on track is no easy task. The following "memory enhancers" can help you to recall your past:

PERSONAL RECORDS

- family albums, photographs, and scrapbooks
- home movies, slides
- diaries and/or business journals
- correspondence (family, friends, business)
- family records in a Bible or other religious book
- birth certificates, adoption records
- baptismal and confirmation certificates
- baby books
- school records (yearbooks, autograph books, diplomas)
- awards
- marriage licenses, wedding invitations
- household records, budget books
- recipes
- passports
- military records
- divorce records
- wills
- death certificates, obituaries, cemetery records
- historical accounts of cities, towns, and countries where you lived

SOUNDS

- birds in the springtime
- wildlife
- loons
- airplanes, helicopters
- motorboats at the lake
- crying
- laughter of family and friends
- children playing
- steam engine
- church bells, chimes
- train whistle
- cars
- Christmas carols and singing
- playing a game of marbles
- slamming of a door
- thunder
- whistling
- musical instruments
- typing
- tap dancing

SMELLS

- burning leaves
- animals
- perfume
- cooking
- men's cologne
- barbequing
- preserves
- holiday baking
- flower gardens
- baby powder
- tobacco
- line-hung washing
- lavender
- farm

TASTES

- home-made pies
- poultry
- jawbreakers
- wild game
- chocolate bars
- porridge
- penny candy
- soft drinks
- fresh garden vegetables
- ice cream
- barbequed meats
- chewing gum
- fruit off a tree
- pastries
- medicine
- chicken soup
- raw rhubarb dipped in sugar
- cookies

FOR FAMILY MEMBERS

Although *Once Upon a Lifetime*... was written to help people record the details of their own lives, it can also be used by family members who want to learn the stories of their parents or grandparents and preserve these memories for the generations to come. If you are working on this type of family history, the following suggestions may be helpful:

- Make sure your family member understands and supports this project before you begin.

- Show him or her this book, and look over the various sections that you would like to talk about. Are there any that seem to be particularly important to your relative, or any that he or she would rather not discuss?

- Ask if your family member can help you to obtain some of the family records listed in the previous section.

- Decide whether you will be taking written notes or using a tape recorder or video camera, and assemble the equipment you need.

- Choose an appropriate time for your conversations. If you are not living with your family member, you may want to call to confirm the time before you arrive.

- Don't plan lengthy sessions, particularly if your relative is elderly. On the other hand, if he or she is eager to talk, you needn't keep to a fixed schedule!

- Use the questions as a guide, but don't hesitate to follow where the interview is leading. Ask additional questions based on the stories you are hearing.

- After you have written out your notes or transcribed a tape-recorded interview, you might want to ask your relative to review the stories, and to clarify some points or add details.

- Remember to thank your family member in some appropriate way, perhaps with a gift such as a framed snapshot of the two of you together.

- Keep in touch, and add new chapters....

This legacy of memories
has been put together by

_____

Date

_____

The Present

Personal Information

1. ☐ What is your full name?

   _____

   _____

2. ☐ Are you married, single, separated, divorced, or widowed?

   _____

   _____

3. ☐ What is your race? Do you talk with an accent?
   How many languages do you speak?

   _____

   _____

4. ☐ Describe yourself physically (hair: color, curly or straight, thin or
   thick; eye color; height; build). Are you right- or left-handed?

   _____

   _____

   _____

   _____

   _____

5. ☐ Do you still have your own teeth, or do you wear dentures?

   _____

   _____

6. ☐ Do you have good eyesight? Do you wear glasses?
   Are you nearsighted or farsighted?

   _____

   _____

7. ☐ Do you have any problems with your hearing? Do you wear an aid?

   _____

   _____

8. ☐ What do you consider your best physical feature? Your worst?
Is there something you would change if you could?

_____

_____

_____

_____

9. ☐ How would you describe your personality (outgoing, shy,
pessimistic, optimistic)? Have you changed very much
since your teenage years?

_____

_____

_____

_____

10. ☐ Is there a personality trait of yours that is dominant throughout
your family?

_____

_____

11. ☐ What kind of clothes do you normally wear during the day? Are
you considered a stylish dresser? When the weekend arrives, what
do you wear to relax?

_____

_____

_____

_____

12. ☐ Have you ever been color-draped? If so, what category are you?
What color of clothes do you usually prefer to buy?

_____

_____

13. ☐ If female, do you like pale or bright lipstick colors? Do you use a lot of make-up? What brand do you usually buy? Do you refuse to go anywhere without your make-up on?

_____

_____

14. ☐ Do you accent your clothes with a lot of jewelry? Do you prefer gold or silver jewelry? What kind of rings do you wear and how many? If married, describe your rings and how they were picked out.

_____

_____

_____

_____

15. ☐ Is there a piece of jewelry you wear daily that you consider "lucky" (for example, a charm or religious symbol)?

_____

_____

16. ☐ Do you have pierced ears? If so, how many earrings do you wear in each ear? What made you decide to pierce your ears and how old were you when you had them done? Do you wear any kind of earrings or prefer good quality gold or silver? Are you allergic to the metals in jewelry?

_____

_____

_____

_____

17. ☐ Have you had any other parts of your body pierced? If so, where? What was the reaction of your family and peers?

_____

_____

18. ☐ Do you have any tatoos? If so, describe them. What made you decide to have tatoos? Have you ever regretted that decision?

_____

_____

_____

19. ☐ How often do you get your hair cut? What does a haircut cost?

_____

_____

20. ☐ Do you color your hair? If so, do you do it yourself or get it done professionally? What colors have you tried?

_____

_____

21. ☐ What kind of shoes do you prefer to wear? Do you stick to the basic colors or are you a person who likes to match your outfits?

_____

_____

22. ☐ Do you ever wear hats? If so, for what reason? Do you like wearing them to sporting events? Are they worn as part of a uniform?

_____

_____

23. ☐ Are you a laid-back or highly-motivated person? Do you procrastinate or feel good about getting things done?

_____

_____

_____

24. ☐ Do you consider yourself a perfectionist? Are you a list maker?

_____

_____

_____

25. ☐   For social events or business appointments are you usually early, on time, or late?

_____

_____

26. ☐   What are your special skills (leadership, organizational)?

_____

_____

_____

_____

27. ☐   Are you ambitious? What goals have you set lately?

_____

_____

_____

28. ☐   Would you describe yourself as a person with character, courage, and conscience?

_____

_____

_____

29. ☐   Do you consider yourself a private person? Are you content being by yourself?

_____

_____

_____

30. ☐   When you want some peace and quiet, where do you go and what do you do?

_____

_____

_____

31. ☐ When weekends arrive, do you spend the time leisurely or are you working at a frantic pace?

32. ☐ What is your favorite way of relaxing? Do you like people around you or prefer to be alone?

33. ☐ Do you have a favorite chair? Where is it?

34. ☐ How many hours of sleep do you try to get each night? Is insomnia your companion? If so, do you read, get out of bed, or just suffer?

35. ☐ What kind of bed do you sleep in? Do you like a lot of blankets, a duvet, or an electric blanket? Do you need a special kind of pillow?

36. ☐ Do you sleep with the window open? If you have a mate, do you have opposing ideas as to how hot or cold a room should be at night?

37. ☐ What do you wear to bed? Has your idea of attire for bed changed over the years? If so, why?

38. ☐ Is it a habit of yours to read before you go to sleep? What do you usually think about before falling asleep?

_____

39. ☐ Do you and/or your spouse snore? Has the snoring required medical intervention? Do either of you have sleep apnea?

_____

_____

40. ☐ Have you made a decision to sleep in separate rooms in order to get a good night's sleep? Is this presenting a problem?

_____

41. ☐ When you arise in the morning, are you alert as your feet hit the floor or does it take a long time for you to wake up?

_____

42. ☐ Are you a shower or bath person? Do you do this in the morning or at night?

_____

_____

Relationships

43. ☐ Do you meet and make friends easily?

_____

_____

44. ☐ Have you ever met someone famous? If so, who?

_____

_____

45. ☐ Who is your best friend? How did you meet? What is so special about this friend? How many years has it been since you first met?

_____

_____

_____

_____

46. ☐ Are there other friends who have been or are a special part of your life? Do you believe it was fate that connected you to them?

_____

_____

_____

_____

47. ☐ Do you share your problems with a lot of people or one specific friend? Do you believe that talking to a friend is just as good as talking to a professional therapist?

_____

_____

_____

48. ☐ Is there someone you talk to on the telephone on a daily basis?

_____

_____

49. ☐ What do you and your friends do when you get together (for example, shop, create crafts, go to social events, discuss business)?

_____

_____

_____

_____

50. ☐ Whom do you trust? Do you find it difficult to trust people? If so, why?

_____

_____

_____

51. ☐ Have you ever been betrayed? If so, what happened?

_____

_____

_____

_____

52. ☐ Do you consider yourself prejudiced? Have you ever felt prejudiced against? If so, describe what happened.

_____

_____

_____

_____

_____

53. ☐ Do you have a pet in your home? If so, what is it? Is there an animal you would never allow in your home? Do you believe that having a pet to care about is good for a person's emotional health?

_____

_____

_____

_____

_____

Your Current Home

54. ☐ What is your present address? How many years have you lived here?

_____

_____

_____

55. ☐ What is the history of the name of your city or town?

_____

_____

_____

56. ☐ Do you live in the suburbs or the city? Would you like to move to a different area?

_____

_____

57. ☐ Do you live in an area with gravel or paved roads? Is it busy or quiet in your neighborhood?

_____

_____

58. ☐ Is there a landmark in your neighborhood that is famous?

_____

_____

59. ☐ Are you near a large shopping center? Do you like the convenience?

_____

_____

60. ☐ Describe your house or apartment (brick or wood; size; exterior color; location). Is your house or apartment modern or traditional?

_____

_____

_____

61. ☐ What colors are prevalent in your decorating theme?

_____

_____

62. ☐ Would you say your decorating is ecclectic or have you a specific look throughout your home?

_____

_____

63. ☐ Describe the view from your front room. Is it one you enjoy?

64. ☐ Do you have any fireplaces? Are you using them as much as you had anticipated? If not, why?

65. ☐ Does your home have a porch or balcony? If so, is it used often?

66. ☐ Describe the view from your kitchen window. Is the kitchen an area where the family gathers frequently?

67. ☐ Which is your favorite room in this home? Why?

68. ☐ Have you ever done a major renovation to your home? Did you find it a stressful undertaking? Did it turn out as you expected?

69. ☐ Is your home used as a gathering place for family and friends? Do you like having a lot of people around you to "break bread" and share time with each other?

_____

_____

_____

70. ☐ Are you concerned about home security? Do you use the services of a security company? Have you installed bars on your windows?

_____

_____

_____

_____

71. ☐ Do you plant a vegetable garden (large or small)? Are these vegetables processed for use during the winter months? Is this something you do because you consider it healthier than buying from the stores?

_____

_____

_____

72. ☐ Does the landscaping in your yard include a lot of flowers and/or shrubs? What kinds and colors do you like? Does working in the yard relax you or is it just a job?

_____

_____

_____

73. ☐ Describe your dream home. Where would it be located?

_____

_____

74. ❐ Are you a "city slicker" or do you prefer country living?

_____

_____

75. ❐ Which buildings come to mind when your city or town is mentioned?

_____

_____

Other Properties

76. ❐ If you own and reside in more than one home during the year, where are they located? How often do you travel to each place?

_____

_____

_____

_____

77. ❐ Describe these dwellings and whether or not you enjoy travelling back and forth.

_____

_____

_____

_____

78. ❐ Do you consider that you live a lavish life filled with all the amenities one would ever desire? If so, do you feel fulfilled?

_____

_____

_____

79. ❐ Do you have a cottage at a lake? Where is it located? How long does it take for you to get to the lake from your house?

_____

80. ☐ Describe the cottage (for example, construction, size, color, lakefront or in the woods).

_____

_____

_____

_____

81. ☐ Are there any special feelings you experience when you visit the cottage? Is this the ultimate form of relaxation for you?

_____

_____

_____

_____

82. ☐ How often do you go to this retreat? Would you like to live there permanently?

_____

_____

83. ☐ What activities do you involve yourself in during your stay?

_____

_____

_____

_____

84. ☐ Do you have all the modern conveniences of home or do you prefer "roughing it"?

_____

_____

85. ☐ Share some interesting thoughts of your trips to the lake that you would like remembered.

_____

_____

_____

_____

86. ☐ Do you live in one area for the summer months and another area for the winter months? What are the merits of this kind of living?

_____

_____

_____

_____

General

87. ☐ Do you have a daily routine? What time do you usually get up in the morning?

_____

_____

_____

88. ☐ If male, do you shave in the shower or another area? Do you use a straight or electric razor?

_____

_____

89. ☐ What do you have for breakfast? Do you eat this meal "on the run" or not at all? Do you start your day with a cup of coffee or tea?

_____

_____

_____

90. ☐ If you could order a favorite breakfast, what would it be? What do you prefer to put on your toast?

_____

_____

91. ☐ If you are employed, do you drink a lot of coffee at work and snack or are you conscientious about eating well?

_____

_____

92. ❏ Do you drink bottled water or do you feel that the water supply where you live is safe and adequate?

_____

_____

93. ❏ Who does most of the housework in your home? Do you consider the distribution of work fair?

_____

_____

_____

94. ❏ What household chores do you like the most? The least?

_____

_____

_____

_____

95. ❏ Are there certain days when you do certain chores such as shopping, washing, and ironing, or are they done as needed?

_____

_____

96. ❏ Do you think that homemaking is easier today than it was years ago?

_____

_____

97. ❏ Do you watch soap operas regularly? Which are your favorite?

_____

_____

98. ❏ What radio programs do you listen to? Do you prefer music or talk shows on the radio? Which one is your favorite? What is your favorite morning show on the radio?

_____

_____

_____

_____

99. ☐ Do you follow the news on radio or television, read it in the newspaper, or receive information from all these sources?

_____

_____

_____

100. ☐ When do you read the newspaper? What part do you read first? What is your favorite paper? Do you read papers from other parts of the world?

_____

_____

_____

_____

101. ☐ Do you use a computer to get news and information? Do you think computers will make newspapers obsolete?

_____

_____

102. ☐ Is reading an important part of your life? Do you read daily? What kind of reading is your top priority?

_____

_____

_____

_____

103. ☐ Can you think of a book you read that has affected your life? If so, what was it and how did it influence you?

_____

_____

_____

_____

104. ☐ What kind of music do you prefer? Do you have music playing in your home regularly? Do you play records, 8-tracks, cassettes, or CDs? Are the machines you use up-to-date or old?

_____

_____

_____

_____

105. ☐ Do you keep in contact with out-of-town friends and relatives by long-distance telephone calls, fax machines, or e-mail, or do you write letters? How much is your average monthly telephone bill?

_____

106. ☐ If your friends and relatives live nearby, how often do you keep in touch?

_____

_____

107. ☐ Is there a parent you telephone daily? Is this done to check on his or her well-being or is it a social call?

_____

108. ☐ Do you use a portable phone? When you are in the car, do you use a cellular phone? If so, is it used more for personal or business calls?

_____

109. ☐ Do you find the telephone distracting and resent the intrusion?

_____

_____

110. ☐ Do you have an annoying habit you are trying to get under control?

_____

_____

111. ☐ What behavior in another person drives you crazy?

_____

_____

112. ☐ Are you a practical joker? Have you ever done anything on April Fool's Day that you thought was hilarious?

_____

_____

113. ☐ Can you describe one of the strangest experiences you have had recently? The funniest?

_____

_____

_____

114. ☐ If you live in a winter climate, what is the coldest temperature you have experienced? Would you like to live in a warmer area?

_____

_____

115. ☐ What industry supports your area? If there is farming, what crops are grown?

_____

_____

116. ☐ What changes have you noticed in people's driving habits? Do you believe it should be mandatory to have another driving test after 65 years of age? Should the driving speed be increased or decreased?

_____

_____

_____

117. ☐ When you are in your car, do you listen to motivational tapes or a radio station or do you prefer silence?

_____

_____

118. ☐ How much does it cost for you to fill up your car with gas?

_____

119. ☐ Is there a charity you support? Why have you chosen this particular charity? If there are several organizations, describe your involvement in each one.

_____

_____

120. ☐ Have you ever been called to jury duty?

_____

121. ☐ Do you ever visit your city hall? If so, for what reason?

_____

122. ☐ Have you ever been elected to office? If so, what was your position? Was this tenure a rewarding experience or very stressful? Would you do it again? If not, why not?

_____

_____

_____

123. ☐ Do you ever write or telephone city officials to complain or make requests? Are you satisfied with their accomplishments?

_____

124. ☐ Are you in agreement with many of the government cutbacks? If not, what are your concerns? How would you do things differently?

_____

_____

125. ☐ Which political party do you support? Has this changed over the years?

_____

_____

126. ☐ Do you like your present prime minister or president? If so, why? If not, why not? Which prime minister or president in the past did you admire the most? Do you think a woman will ever be elected to this office?

_____

_____

127. ☐ Where were you when President Kennedy died? Describe your feelings.

_____

128. ☐ Where were you and how did you feel when you heard about the death of Diana, Princess of Wales?

_____

_____

_____

_____

Cooking and Food

129. ☐ What are some of the things you have learned about food shopping? Are you a coupon user? How much money do you save using them?

_____

_____

_____

_____

130. ☐ Do you have a separate account for food money? Are you noticing your food budget shrinking?

_____

131. ☐ What is your monthly grocery bill (approximately)? Did/do you run short of food money at times? Did/do you ever use a food bank?

_____

_____

132. ☐ Where do you usually buy your groceries (chain store near you, discount superstores, convenience stores)? Do you ever phone in your grocery order? Would you order food by computer?

_____

133. ☐ Do you like to cook? What is your favorite recipe?

_____

134. ☐ When preparing meals, do you change your menu often or do you follow a routine?

_____

135. ☐ What method of cooking do you enjoy using (stove-top, oven, microwave, barbeque, stir-fry, pressure cooking, steaming, crockery)?

_____

136. ☐ Do you have gas or electric appliances?

_____

137. ☐ Do you eat meals at the same time every day? If so, when? Do you sit down at the table to eat or eat casually in front of the television?

_____

138. ☐ Is there a special meal that you have eaten that stands out in your memory? Do you love gourmet food or are you a "meat and potato" person?

_____

_____

_____

139. ☐ Is there any food you cannot tolerate? Are you allergic to any food?

_____

_____

_____

140. ☐ If you were to order your last meal on earth, what would it be? What would you drink with your last meal?

_____

_____

Social Activities

141. ☐ What do you do socially during the week?

_____

_____

142. ☐ Are you a participant in sports? Which ones? How many hours each week does this occupy your time? If not a participant, which sports do you enjoy watching, if any?

_____

_____

_____

_____

143. ☐ Do you travel to different areas to support your local sports teams?

_____

_____

144. ☐ Who are your local sports heroes? Have you met any of them personally?

_____

_____

145. ☐ Is there conflict in your home due to the priority placed on sports?

_____

_____

146. ☐ Who is your favorite sports announcer? Why?

_____

_____

147. ☐ Do you enjoy attending live theatre? Art galleries? Museums? Space science centers? Was this appreciation nurtured since you were a small child?

_____

_____

_____

_____

148. ☐ What kind of parties do you like to attend or host? How often? What kind of music do you prefer at these events?

_____

_____

149. ☐ Do you enjoy dancing? What is your favorite dance? What is the latest dance craze?

_____

_____

_____

150. ☐ Do you like to go hiking or bird watching with others? If so, where do you go?

_____

_____

151. ☐ Do you go to gambling casinos? How often? Do you play the lotteries? Have you ever won?

_____

_____

Technology

152. ☐ What do you think about the new technology in our world today? Do you resist it or have you embraced it as a challenge?

_____

_____

153. ☐ What is your most recently acquired electronic gadget?

_____

154. ☐ How many television sets do you have in your home? How many hours do you spend each day watching programs?

_____

_____

155. ☐ What new invention do you not want in your home?

_____

_____

156. ☐ Are you computer literate? If so, do you spend a lot of time on the Internet? Do you use the Internet as a resource or is it strictly for fun and chat lines? Have you met friends through this medium?

_____

_____

157. ☐ Have you made the transition to the ATMs at the banks? Do you resent the fact that there is less personal contact at these facilities?

_____

_____

Finances

158. ☐ Are you considered a good money manager? If so, have you passed this skill on to your family? What saving system do you use?

_____

_____

_____

159. ☐ Who handles the money in your family? Does this arrangement work out well?

_____

_____

160. ☐ Do you make a point of saving for the future? If not, how are you going to finance your future?

_____

_____

_____

_____

161. ☐ Have you ever had a serious financial setback? If so, what happened?

_____

_____

_____

_____

162. ☐ Was there ever a time when you put money into an investment and "lost your shirt?" If so, what happened? Did you become more cautious after that experience?

_____

_____

_____

_____

163. ☐ Was there ever a time you had to help out your family financially? What happened? Did you have to look after your parents? Is this your situation now?

_____

_____

_____

_____

164. ☐ We've read that many rich people are not happy. Do you believe that money is "the root of all evil"?

_____

_____

Holidays, Travel, and Special Occasions

165. ☐ Do you welcome your birthday or dread its arrival? Why?

_____

_____

166. ☐ Which has been your most memorable birthday? Why?

_____

_____

_____

167. ☐ How did you celebrate your milestone birthdays: 13th? 16th? 21st? 30th? 40th? 50th? 65th? 75th? 85th? *Use your journal or notebook.*

_____

_____

_____

168. ☐ Did you have a special Bar Mitzvah or Bat Mitzvah? What did you do and where was it held?

_____

_____

_____

169. ☐ Do you like to send and receive cards for all occasions? Are you good at remembering birthdays? Do you have a special birthday book or does someone always have to remind you?

_____

_____

_____

170. ☐ When it comes to gift giving, do you buy something you feel the recipient would like or do you buy what's on sale at the last moment?

_____

_____

171. ☐ Are you one of those people who purchase gifts months ahead of time? Why do you buy this way?

_____

_____

172. ☐ Are there any special days celebrated or remembered by you alone?

_____

_____

173. ☐ Is Valentine's Day important to you? Do you send cards to family and friends? Do you consider yourself a romantic person? What have you done with your mate on this date that is extra special?

_____

_____

_____

_____

174. ☐ At Easter time, do you gather in your home or visit family elsewhere? What traditions do you follow? Do you make an Easter tree?

_____

_____

_____

_____

175. ☐ Is Mother's Day and/or Father's Day important to you? If you are adopted, do you ever think of your biological parents on this day? If you are the biological parent, do you think about the child you gave up for adoption? Describe your feelings.

_____

_____

_____

_____

176. ☐ Is Thanksgiving one of the most important celebrations of your year? What traditions do you follow? What meal do you prefer? Do you entertain the family in your home or usually travel elsewhere?

_____

_____

_____

_____

_____

177. ☐ Do you have a lot of children at your door for Halloween? What treats do you usually give out? If you have attended costume parties, what is the best outfit you remember wearing?

_____

_____

_____

_____

_____

178. ☐ How do you spend Christmas or Hanukkah? Is it similar to when you were a child? What traditions do you follow? What does this occasion mean to you?

_____

_____

_____

_____

179. ☐ Is there a different religious ritual that you celebrate? Describe it and what it means to you and your family.

_____

_____

_____

180. ☐ How do you spend New Year's or Rosh Hashanah? What traditions do you follow? What year do you remember as being the best celebration?

_____

_____

_____

_____

181. ☐ Is it a New Year's Day tradition for you to watch the Rose Bowl Parade?

_____

_____

182. ☐ Does one particular holiday gift stand out in your mind? What was it and when did you receive it?

_____

_____

183. ☐ Do you remember being alone on a special holiday? What happened?

_____

_____

184. ☐ When do you like to take your vacation?

_____

_____

185. ☐ What vacation did you enjoy the most? Where did you go?

_____

_____

_____

186. ☐ Did you ever take a holiday that turned out to be a disaster? If so, what happened?

_____

_____

187. ☐ Have you ever gone to Europe? If not, would you like to go? What countries have you visited? Which one was your favorite?

_____

_____

_____

_____

188. ☐ Have you ever been on a cruise? If so, how many times? What was your destination? Was it one of your favorite ways to travel?

_____

_____

_____

_____

189. ☐ When was your first airplane flight? Where did you go? Were you nervous? Have you ever experienced an airplane tragedy?

_____

_____

_____

190. ☐ Have you ever travelled by train? Was this a memorable experience? Describe your trip. Would you like to do this again?

_____

_____

_____

_____

191. ☐ Have you ever taken a trip on a motorbike? If so, where?

_____

_____

192. ☐ Do you own a Harley-Davidson? If so, is this the ultimate way to travel, as far as you're concerned? Where have you gone?

_____

_____

_____

193. ☐ Do you like camping? Where have you gone?

_____

_____

_____

_____

194. ☐ Do trips to the mountains rank as one of your favorite holidays? If so, where do you go and why?

_____

_____

_____

_____

195. ☐ When someone mentions taking a holiday, do you envision being by the sea as your first choice? If so, why?

_____

_____

_____

196. ☐ Is the perfect holiday for you just staying at home and visiting local areas? Why?

_____

_____

197. ☐ While away on vacation, are you continually taking pictures?

_____

_____

198. ☐ Have you ever been sick on a holiday? In a foreign country? What happened?

_____

_____

_____

_____

199. ☐ Were you ever caught without enough health insurance in another country? If so, what happened?

_____

_____

_____

200. ☐ Have you ever taken a trip alone? Where? Would you do it again?

_____

_____

_____

201. ☐ Do you vacation with your children or grandchildren? If so, where do you like to go?

_____

_____

_____

202. ☐ What kind of souvenirs do you usually bring home?

_____

_____

_____

203. ☐ Are you somone who enjoys getting away on a holiday but always looks forward to coming home?

_____

_____

204. ☐ Is there a special place you'd love to visit again? If money were no object, where in the world would you go for a vacation?

_____

_____

_____

Health

205. ☐ Do you consider yourself healthy? If so, is it because you are conscious of what you eat and take measures to ensure a good quality of life? Describe.

_____

_____

_____

206. ☐ If you are not healthy, what has happened? Do you feel your condition has been inherited? Are you negligent about your health?

_____

_____

_____

207. ☐ Do you have a disease or handicap that requires constant care and attention? If so, describe your feelings.

_____

_____

_____

_____

208. ☐ Do you have medical conditions that require you to take
medication? What are they and what do you take? Do you suffer
from depression?

_____

_____

_____

_____

209. ☐ Do you have medical conditions that were not discovered until later
in life? If so, what are they?

_____

_____

210. ☐ Have you suffered silently or openly with fears and/or phobias?
Describe them. Have you been able to control them or do you
conceal them?

_____

_____

_____

_____

211. ☐ Do you get colds on a regular basis? How do you treat your colds?

_____

_____

_____

212. ☐ Medications have greatly improved over the years. Do you
remember when Dr. Salk invented the polio vaccine? When
penicillin was discovered, do you recall the excitement?

_____

_____

213. ☐ What health history do you want your family to be aware of (allergies, diseases, accidents, operations, or surgical procedures)?

_____

_____

_____

_____

214. ☐ Do you think the food we eat is healthy? Why or why not?

_____

215. ☐ Do you subscribe to the holistic approach for well-being? Do you watch your fat intake? Are you a garlic eater? Are there certain foods you eat that you are convinced have added extra years to your life?

_____

_____

_____

_____

216. ☐ Do you take vitamins on a daily basis? Which ones?

_____

_____

217. ☐ How often do you visit a doctor? Are you diligent about getting yearly exams? Do you ever visit a chiropractor?

_____

_____

_____

218. ☐   Is physical exercise an important part of your daily life?

_____

_____

_____

_____

219. ☐   Do you run? If so, how far each day? Have you ever entered a marathon? Did you win anything? Do you use a personal trainer? What time of day do you like to exercise?

_____

_____

_____

_____

220. ☐   Do you go to a health spa on a regular basis? What equipment do you use? Do you use exercise videos for a workout at home?

_____

_____

_____

221. ☐   Are you a yoga enthusiast? Do you meditate? Are there any forms or techniques of relaxation for your body and/or soul that you like?

_____

_____

_____

_____

222. ☐   Do you consider yourself more energetic or more conservative than most of your friends?

_____

_____

223. ☐ Have you noticed any changes in yourself, both physically and mentally, over the past few years?

_____

_____

_____

_____

224. ☐ Have you had to curtail certain activities due to poor health?

_____

_____

225. ☐ Have you ever been addicted to anything? If so, what? Have you managed to overcome this addiction? Describe what happened.

_____

_____

_____

_____

_____

226. ☐ Have you ever dieted? If so, name the diets you have tried. Did you attain your goal and remain there? If not, what happened?

_____

_____

_____

_____

_____

227. ☐ What would you describe as the benefits and joys of reaching middle age? Are you concerned about aging?

_____

_____

_____

228. ☐ Did you experience a mid-life crisis? When and where? Did you notice a change in your appearance at that time (gray hair or wrinkles)? Was it at this time that you started thinking of mortality?

_____

_____

_____

_____

229. ☐ If you are a female, have you reached menopause? If so, at what age did it happen? What symptoms did/do you experience? Did/do you take estrogen supplements? Were/are you much more sensitive and in turmoil? Did/does your family comment on your behavior? What advice would you give to women going through menopause?

_____

_____

_____

_____

230. ☐ Do you think too much emphasis is being put on a woman's figure and youthfulness?

_____

_____

231. ☐ So many people say they are "stressed" these days and that their nerves are worn out. Have you ever had or felt like you were going to have a nervous breakdown? If so, what caused those feelings? Have you been able to stabilize yourself? If so, how?

_____

_____

_____

_____

232. ☐ Have you ever tried to commit suicide? If so, what happened to bring you to that point? If you have considered such an action, what made you change your mind? Have you visited a psychologist or psychiatrist to resolve problems?

_____

_____

_____

Disasters and Crime

233. ☐ Have you ever lost your possessions in a fire, storm, earthquake, or other disaster? If so, how did you gather the courage to continue?

_____

_____

_____

_____

234. ☐ Have you been a victim of crime? When and how did this happen?

_____

_____

_____

_____

235. ☐ Do you think the crime we are experiencing today is due, in part, to both parents having to work and thus being unable to spend as much time with their children? Is television a bad influence? Do you believe drugs play a role in the crime statistics?

_____

_____

_____

_____

236. ☐ Are you afraid of being robbed, having your car hijacked, being sexually molested, or going out alone? How do you protect yourself?

_____

_____

_____

_____

237. ☐ Do you feel safe where you live or would you like to move?

_____

_____

238. ☐ Were you ever issued a speeding ticket? If so, when and where? Have you ever been in a car accident? If so, what happened? Were you negligent? Are you more diligent about driving habits now?

_____

_____

_____

_____

_____

239. ☐ Were there ever any incidents in your life when someone saved you from a terrible mishap? If so, what happened?

_____

_____

_____

_____

_____

240. ☐ Do you believe in the death penalty? Why or why not?

_____

_____

_____

241. ☐ If you lived during the Great Depression of the 1930s, do you remember its impact on your family? Do you believe that either living through the Depression or hearing of hardships endured by your family has affected your decisions over the years?

_____

_____

_____

_____

_____

242. ☐ Do you believe that the world is currently in danger of a nuclear war? In your opinion, do you feel this could mean the end of the world?

_____

_____

Religion and Psychic and Scientific Phenomena

243. ☐ Do you believe in God? Do you pray? Do you attend church on a regular basis? What religion or faith do you embrace?

_____

_____

_____

_____

244. ☐ Is there a specific religious program you watch on television or listen to on radio that takes the place of attending church?

_____

_____

245. ☐ If you are an agnostic, why do you feel that way?

_____

_____

_____

246. ☐ Were you affected by the death of Mother Teresa? If so, how?

_____

_____

_____

247. ☐ Has something happened in your life that you believe could only have been a miracle? If so, what was your experience?

_____

_____

_____

_____

_____

248. ☐ Do you believe in reincarnation? When people die, do you think they go to Heaven? Do you expect to see your parents and loved ones in an afterlife? If not, what do you believe?

_____

_____

_____

_____

249. ☐ Have you ever had a premonition about something before it happened? Do you feel that you are psychic? Are you a person who "trusts your gut feeling"?

_____

_____

_____

_____

250. ☐ What are some of the family superstitions you believe and/or some new ones that you have acquired?

_____

_____

_____

_____

251. ☐ Do you believe in astrology? Have you ever had your chart read? What sign are you?

_____

_____

_____

_____

252. ☐ Have you ever played with a ouija board? Did anything happen? Have you ever attended a séance? If so, describe what happened. If not, do you think you would ever get involved in one?

_____

_____

_____

253. ☐ Do you believe that there is life in outer space? Do you believe that aliens are or have been on earth? Have you ever seen a flying saucer? Are you interested in this subject? Would you like to take a trip in outer space?

_____

_____

_____

_____

_____

Feelings about Life

254. ☐ Have your values and beliefs changed over the years? What do you value most in life?

_____

_____

_____

255. ☐ Are you a realist or a dreamer? Is this a good thing for you?

_____

_____

256. ☐ What do you do to attain peace of mind?

_____

_____

_____

_____

257. ☐ What makes you feel happy? What makes you feel sad?

_____

_____

_____

258. ☐ Do you ever feel lonely? What contributes to those feelings?

_____

_____

_____

259. ☐ When did you learn to assume responsibility for yourself? How did it happen?

_____

_____

_____

260. ☐ What do you think was/were the turning point/s in your life? How did your life change after this/these event/s?

_____

_____

_____

261. ☐ Was there a time you thought you should have made a different choice in your life?

262. ☐ What are your personal feelings about life itself and its purpose?

263. ☐ What has been life's biggest surprise?

264. ☐ What has been your biggest challenge in life?
How did you handle it?

265. ☐ Do you feel that life has been a struggle? If so, why?

266. ☐ Is there something you have accomplished in your life that has given you a lot of pride (for example, overcoming an addiction, losing weight, quitting smoking, raising children, or learning a language)?

267. ☐ Have you felt cheated in life insofar as time, money, love, or family is concerned? If so, what happened to make you feel this way?

_____

_____

_____

_____

268. ☐ What has been your biggest disappointment in life so far?

_____

_____

_____

269. ☐ When was the most satisfying time of your life? Why? When was the least satisfying time of your life? Why?

_____

_____

_____

270. ☐ What makes you angry? Do you fly into a rage easily? How do you handle your temper?

_____

_____

_____

_____

271. ☐ Are there fears you carry with you on a regular basis? What are they and how do you deal with them?

_____

_____

_____

272. ☐ What is your "pet peeve"?

_____

_____

273. ☐ Have you noticed that what you once thought was important in life is no longer important? If so, what are some of these areas?

_____

_____

_____

_____

274. ☐ What was the kindest thing you ever did for someone else? What was the kindest thing someone else did for you?

_____

_____

_____

275. ☐ Who was the one person who had the most impact on your life? What was it that made this individual so special?

_____

_____

_____

276. ☐ If you could be anybody in the world, who would it be? Why?

_____

_____

277. ☐ How do you reminisce (photos, stories, videos, movies, slides, letters)?

_____

_____

_____

278. ☐ Do you find yourself living in the past? Is that a good idea?

_____

_____

_____

279. ☐ Have you kept a family secret that no one else knows of? Why?

_____

_____

_____

_____

280. ☐ Is there something in your past that you will never tell anyone
about? If so, why have you made this choice?

_____

_____

_____

_____

281. ☐ Is the world today moving too fast for you? What areas concern or
confuse you?

_____

_____

_____

_____

282. ☐ What worries you about the future?

_____

_____

_____

_____

283. ☐ When was your first experience with death? How did you deal with the loss?

_____

_____

_____

_____

284. ☐ What are your feelings about dying? Would you prefer to die at home or in a hospital?

_____

_____

_____

_____

285. ☐ Has someone close to you died recently? Who was it and how did this death affect you?

_____

_____

_____

_____

286. ☐ Did you ever seek out grief counselling? If so, was it helpful?

_____

_____

287. ☐ Are members of your family buried in your city or town? Do you visit the cemetery on a regular basis or on special days?

_____

_____

_____

288. ☐ Have you ensured that your will and Enduring Power of Attorney forms have been finalized to assist your family when the time arises? If not, why not?

_____

289. ☐ What would you like your epitaph to be?
_____
_____
_____

290. ☐ If you had your life to live all over again, would you do anything differently? If so, what?
_____
_____
_____
_____
_____

291. ☐ What is it you would still like to accomplish in life?
_____
_____

292. ☐ What do you believe is the key to happiness?
_____
_____

Some of the above questions are duplicated in the Retirement section. If you are not now retired, the questions in the Retirement section may be answered differently once you retire.

The following are some questions regarding your "personal favorites":

293. ☐ What is your favorite color?
_____

294. ☐ What is your favorite flower?
_____

295. ☐ What is your favorite book? Magazine?
_____

296. ☐ Who is your favorite author?

297. ☐ Who is your favorite political representative?

298. ☐ What is your favorite kind of art work?

299. ☐ Who is your favorite artist?

300. ☐ What is your favorite kind of music?

301. ☐ What is your favorite song?

302. ☐ Who is your favorite singer?

303. ☐ What is your favorite sport?

304. ☐ Who is your favorite player in that sport?

305. ☐ What is your favorite time of day?

306. ☐ What is your favorite thing to do on a night out?

307. ☐ What is your favorite cookbook?

308. ☐ What is your favorite meal?

309. ☐ What is your favorite dessert?

310. ☐ What is your favorite pizza topping?

311. ☐ What is your favorite fast-food order?

312. ☐ What is your favorite fruit?

313. ☐ What is your favorite vegetable?

314. ☐ What is your favorite soup?

315. ☐ What is your favorite snack?

316. ☐ What is your favorite candy?

317. ☐ What is your favorite kind of cake?

318. ☐ What is your favorite flavor of ice-cream?

319. ☐ What is your favorite perfume?

320. ☐ What is your favorite after-shave and/or cologne?

321. ☐ What is your favorite movie?

322. ☐ Who is your favorite actress? Actor?

323. ☐ What is your favorite television program?

324. ☐ Who is your favorite comedian/comedienne?

325. ☐ What is your favorite cartoon (in the newspaper or on television)?

326. ☐ What is your favorite season?

327. ☐ What is your favorite family holiday?

328. ☐ Where is your favorite area for a winter vacation?

329. ☐ What is your favorite animal and/or pet?

330. ☐ What was your favorite age?

331. ☐ What is your favorite piece of jewelry?

332. ☐ What is your favorite new invention for the kitchen?

333. ☐ What is a favorite joke you'd like to share?

Memories of
Childhood

334. ☐ What was your full given name at birth?

_____

_____

335. ☐ When were you born (month, day, year)?

_____

_____

336. ☐ In what city/town/country and hospital were you born?

_____

_____

337. ☐ Were you named after someone? If so, who? If not, how was your name chosen?

_____

_____

338. ☐ What did you weigh at birth? How many inches in length were you?

_____

_____

339. ☐ Do you know whether you had any health problems when you were born? If so, what were they?

_____

_____

_____

340. ☐ Were you baptised? When and where? Who are/were your godparents?

_____

_____

_____

341. ☐ Were you given a nickname? If so, who started calling you by that name and why?

_____

_____

_____

_____

342. ☐ What did you look like as a child (tall, short, thin, heavy)?

343. ☐ What were you like (serious, quiet, sad, happy, outgoing, shy)?

344. ☐ Did you have the usual childhood diseases? List the ones that you can remember. Are you aware of any complications resulting from those diseases?

345. ☐ What diseases were people afraid of getting when you were a child?

346. ☐ Were you taken to the doctor's office often due to illness? If so, why were you under a doctor's care?

347. ☐ Were you ever in an accident that required you to be hospitalized?

348. ☐ Can you remember a favorite toy from your childhood? Was there one that was a "security blanket"? Do you still have it?

349. ☐ Were there other toys that you remember fondly?

350. ☐ Was there something special you wanted as a child and never received (for example, a special toy, love from a family member, more friends)?

_____

_____

_____

351. ☐ Did you have to go without things that your friends had when you were growing up? Did you resent the fact they had more than you?

_____

_____

_____

352. ☐ What special treats did you receive from your parents?

_____

_____

_____

353. ☐ What do you remember about Valentine's Day? Did you enjoy receiving cards from your classmates? Were you concerned that you might not get many cards?

_____

_____

_____

_____

354. ☐ What do you remember about Easter? Did anyone hide eggs or make an Easter tree? Was the Easter church service a special family event? Did relatives get together? What did you eat?

_____

_____

_____

_____

_____

355. ☐ What do you remember about Halloween? Did you trick-or-treat or have a home party? Did a family member make you costumes or were they store bought? What kind of treats do you remember getting? Did you get sick from eating so much candy?

_____

_____

_____

_____

_____

356. ☐ Describe Christmas in your childhood home. Did you chop down your own tree or buy one? Who decorated your tree and do you remember what it looked like? Were the ornaments home-made or bought?

_____

_____

_____

_____

357. ☐ Where did you hang your Christmas stocking? Describe any rituals you had regarding Santa Claus, such as writing a letter, or leaving out food.

_____

_____

_____

_____

_____

_____

358. ☐ Was it a custom to open gifts at night or in the morning? Did you have a specific tradition for stocking stuffers? Was your family able to afford presents? If not, what do you remember happening? Conversely, do you feel you had far too many presents?

_____

_____

_____

_____

359. ☐ Was it a tradition for you to attend church on Christmas Eve? Was it a candlelight service? What do you remember about this special night?

_____

_____

_____

_____

360. ☐ What did you eat for your main meal? Did everyone in the family take part in the preparation of this food? If you had turkey, who carved it?

_____

_____

_____

_____

361. ☐ At what age did you discover there was no Santa Claus? How did it happen?

_____

_____

_____

362. ☐ Describe Hanukkah in your childhood home. What traditions did you follow? What did this celebration mean to you at that time? Did family members gather in your home? Was there special music you remember playing or singing?

_____

_____

_____

_____

363. ☐ Was there one present that stands out in your mind? Who gave it to you and why was it so special?

_____

_____

_____

364. ☐ Who were the childhood friends that you played with most of the time? What do you remember doing with them? Are you still in contact with any of those friends?

_____

_____

_____

_____

365. ☐ What childhood games do you remember playing (for example, jacks, marbles, red light, snakes and ladders, hopscotch, skip rope)?

_____

_____

_____

_____

366. ☐ Did you belong to Cubs or Brownies? If so, did you enjoy this experience?

_____

_____

367. ☐ Were you a collector (of sports cards, marbles, comic books, dolls, stamps, or coins, for example)? If so, what did you do with your collection?

_____

_____

_____

368. ☐ What was it like going to movies during your childhood? What were the theaters like? How often did you go? What kind of movie did you prefer (comedy, horror, musical, drama, cartoons)? How much did it cost you to go to a movie?

_____

_____

_____

_____

_____

369. ☐ What was your favorite radio show and/or television show during your childhood? Were you restricted to certain hours of viewing?

_____

_____

_____

370. ☐ Did you learn to play a musical instrument? If so, what kind? Did you learn reluctantly or did you enjoy it? Describe whether or not music is an important part of your life today.

_____

_____

_____

_____

371. ❑ What chores were you required to do as you grew up? Which chores did you dislike the most?

_____

_____

_____

372. ❑ How were you disciplined? In your view, was the discipline fair?

_____

_____

373. ❑ Did you ride a bicycle? If so, how old were you when you received your first bike? Do you remember what it looked like?

_____

_____

374. ❑ Did you roller skate or ice skate? If so, how old were you when you learned how? Describe the ice skating rink you used as a child.

_____

_____

_____

_____

375. ❑ What was your mode of travel (by streetcar, car, bus, train, walking)? Did your parents own a car?

_____

_____

_____

_____

376. ❑ Did you attend Sunday School? What church did you attend? What influence did religion have on you?

_____

_____

_____

377. ☐ What did you want to be when you grew up?

_____

_____

Childhood Home

378. ☐ Do you remember the address of your childhood home?

_____

_____

379. ☐ What did your home look like (color, size, construction)? Did you have a veranda or front porch?

_____

_____

_____

_____

_____

380. ☐ Were you proud of your home or shy about having friends over?

_____

_____

381. ☐ Did you grow up in the same town or city that you were born in? If so, how many years did you live there?

_____

_____

382. ☐ Describe the street where you lived. Were the roads paved or gravelled?

_____

_____

_____

383. ☐ Were there landmarks in your neighborhood that you remember?

_____

_____

_____

_____

384. ☐ What do you remember about your neighbors? Were they friendly? Can you remember a lot of them by name?

_____

_____

_____

_____

385. ☐ Did your family socialize with the neighbors on weekends?

_____

_____

386. ☐ Where was your favorite area of your home? Why?

_____

_____

387. ☐ Do you remember a member of the family sitting in a specific room? Who comes to mind and what were they doing? In which room did the family relax?

_____

_____

_____

_____

388. ☐ Was there a lot of music in your home (either a radio or a musical instrument)? Describe what you remember.

_____

_____

_____

_____

389. ☐ Do you remember your home as being quiet or the "hub of activity"?

_____

_____

390. ☐ Were you allowed to bring your friends home for visits? Describe what you did.

391. ☐ When you sat down as a family for meals in your home, what do you remember talking about? Did you say grace or a blessing?

392. ☐ Did your parents entertain in their home? If so, can you remember what their parties were like?

393. ☐ Was there an area in the house that scared you? Did you have the childhood fear of "monsters under the bed"? If so, describe that fear.

394. ☐ What magazines and/or books do you remember seeing around the home? Was reading encouraged by your parents? Do you remember your parents reading bedtime stories to you?

_____

_____

_____

_____

395. ☐ Did you have electricity? If not, how did you light the rooms? Can you remember when electricity was installed in your home?

_____

_____

396. ☐ How was your home heated? Was your home cold during the winter months? What kind of bedding was used?

_____

_____

_____

397. ☐ Was water rationed at home? How often did you bathe and wash your hair? Do you remember having to warm the water on a stove first and then pour it into a portable tub? If so, describe that experience.

_____

_____

_____

_____

398. ☐ Did your mother use a wringer washer to do the laundry? Do you remember the fresh smell of clothes that were hung outside to dry?

_____

_____

_____

399. ☐ Describe what a telephone looked like and how it was used when you were a child. Were you on a party line?

_____

_____

_____

400. ☐ Did you have a bathroom or an outhouse? If you used an outhouse, were you familiar with the catalogue pages? How old were you when indoor plumbing arrived?

_____

_____

_____

401. ☐ Did your family lock the doors or leave them unlocked? Describe what kind of locks were used.

_____

_____

_____

402. ☐ How was the cooking done in your childhood home (on a wood, electric, or gas stove)?

_____

_____

_____

403. ☐ What appliances do you remember back then? Did you have an ice box or a refrigerator?

_____

_____

_____

404. ☐ Can you describe the dishes your family used?

_____

_____

405. ☐ Do you remember the ice man coming weekly? Did you have milk delivered by horse and wagon or truck? Describe what you remember.

_____

_____

_____

_____

406. ☐ Was there a big vegetable garden in your back yard? What vegetables do you remember your family growing? Did your mother spend many hours preserving food?

_____

_____

_____

_____

407. ☐ What kind of flowers do you remember your family growing? Who in your family did the gardening and outdoor work?

_____

_____

_____

_____

408. ☐ Were there a lot of birds in your yard? Did you have bird houses on your property? What kinds of birds were attracted to your area?

_____

_____

_____

_____

409. ☐ Was it common to have sand boxes and swing sets in your yard?

_____

410. ☐ Was your yard open or did you have a fence or hedge?

_____

411. ☐ What did your family do on Sundays? Did you attend church regularly? Was it a family day when you had family and/or friends over for a meal or simply a leisure day?

_____

_____

_____

412. ☐ Do you look back on your childhood home with happy memories?

_____

413. ☐ What happened to your childhood home? Do any family members still live in it?

_____

_____

_____

If you lived in more than one house during your childhood years, you can re-use questions 378 to 413 to document those memories. This is the time for you to use your journal or notebook.

Teenage Years

414. ☐ What were you like as a teenager? Did you follow the trends of the time (dress, hair, language)?

_____

_____

_____

415. ☐ What did you like or dislike about yourself at that time?

_____

_____

_____

416. ☐ What was a big issue during your teen years (for example, zoot suits)?

_____

_____

_____

417. ☐ How did you celebrate your 16th birthday?

_____

_____

_____

_____

418. ☐ Who was your best friend during those years? Are you still friends?

_____

_____

419. ☐ Did you resent authority? Were you ever "grounded"? If so, why?

_____

_____

_____

420. ☐ Did you ever run away from home or have thoughts of doing so?

_____

_____

421. ☐ Were you given an allowance? If so, were you required to work for it? How much money did you receive and how was it spent?

_____

_____

_____

_____

422. ☐ Were you employed during your teenage years? If so, what did you do? Did you work only during the summer months or on a regular basis? How much money did you make on a weekly basis?

_____

_____

_____

_____

423. ☐ Did you have any hobby that was important to you? How and when did you get interested in that hobby? Are you still involved in that hobby today?

_____

_____

_____

424. ☐ Was there a pet in your home that was special? What was it and what was its name? How many years did the pet live?

_____

_____

_____

425. ☐ Did you have a bedroom of your own? If so, was it a retreat where you spent a lot of time reading and doing homework? What did your room look like? If you had to share with a sibling, where did you escape for solitude?

_____

_____

_____

_____

426. ☐ How many hours of sleep did you usually require, in those days?

_____

_____

427. ☐ Did you keep a diary? What happened to it?

428. ☐ Was there some secret you kept from your parents? If so, what was it, and did you ever tell them about it in later years?

429. ☐ What do you remember about New Year's Eve? Was it a big event for your parents? Did you bring in the New Year with them? Did you always make a "New Year's resolution"?

430. ☐ What do you remember about Rosh Hashanah? Did you get the feeling of family unity? What traditions did you follow?

431. ☐ Who were your idols during your teenage years (for example, sports and movie stars, singers)? Did you ever meet any idols?

432. ❐ Where did teenagers go after school? Was there a favorite
restaurant where everyone gathered? If so, what was it called?

_____

_____

_____

433. ❐ Do you remember what it was like in a restaurant when you were
young (stools and counters, soda fountains, jukeboxes, waitresses'
uniforms)? Describe one of your favorites.

_____

_____

_____

_____

434. ❐ Did you ever attend any rock concerts? If so, who performed?

_____

_____

435. ❐ Did you ever attend a professional theatrical performance such as a
play or musical? Do you still enjoy this type of entertainment?

_____

_____

_____

436. ❐ How did you spend your summer months? Did you go to summer
camp, spend time at a lake or resort, visit relatives, or work?

_____

_____

_____

_____

437. ▢ Did you ever belong to an organization such as Boy Scouts or Girl Guides? What did you learn?

_____

_____

_____

438. ▢ Were you active socially on the weekends? Did you like to go to dances? If so, where were they held (school, community hall, club, dance hall)? What kind of dancing did you do then, and what kind of music did you enjoy?

_____

_____

_____

_____

_____

439. ▢ At what age did you start dating? Were your parents strict about the time you were to be home? Where did you go on dates?

_____

_____

_____

_____

440. ▢ Were you allowed to use the family car for special occasions? What time was your curfew?

_____

_____

441. ▢ Who taught you to drive? How old were you when you got your driver's license?

_____

_____

442. ▢ What was your first car? What color was it? Do you remember what it cost? How much was a tank of gas?

_____

_____

443. ❏ Who was your first love? Describe your first kiss (where, when)?

_____

_____

_____

444. ❏ Did you go steady during your teenage years or "play the field"?
Why did you make that choice?

_____

_____

445. ❏ Who explained the "facts of life" to you? How old were you? Was
sex a forbidden subject?

_____

_____

446. ❏ Did you ever get pregnant and have to give a child up for adoption?
If so, how did that affect you over the years?

_____

_____

_____

_____

447. ❏ Were you afraid of sexually-transmitted diseases during your
teenage years? What birth control was available at that time?

_____

_____

448. ❏ Did you smoke and/or drink as a teenager? Did it become a
lifelong habit?

_____

_____

449. ☐ What political figure and/or member of the royal family do you remember from your teenage years?

_____

_____

_____

_____

450. ☐ Was there something that happened in your teenage years that had a huge impact on you (happy, embarrassing, sad)?

_____

_____

_____

_____

451. ☐ At what age did you leave home? How did you support yourself?

_____

_____

_____

_____

452. ☐ As you look back, would you say your teenage years were your most difficult ones or quite rewarding?

_____

_____

_____

_____

453. ☐ Was there a significant change in your lifestyle once you became an adult and were independent?

_____

_____

_____

_____

Memories of
School Days

Elementary School

454. ☐ Did you attend kindergarten or pre-school before starting Grade 1?

_____

455. ☐ What year did you start Grade 1? Where did you live at this time?

_____

456. ☐ Did you attend a public, separate, or private school? Where?

_____

457. ☐ How far was your elementary school from your home? Did you walk, ride a bus, or get driven to school?

_____

458. ☐ Can you describe your first day of school? Who was your teacher?

_____

_____

_____

_____

459. ☐ Did you wear a uniform? If so, what did it look like?

_____

460. ☐ Did you start your school day with a prayer? Did you pledge allegiance to the flag?

_____

_____

_____

461. ☐ What did your school look like (large or small; made of brick or wood)?

_____

_____

_____

_____

462. ☐ What did a typical classroom look like (desks, coatrooms, lockers)?

_____

_____

_____

_____

463. ☐ Do you remember approximately how many students were in your classes? Were some of the grades combined?

_____

_____

_____

464. ☐ What was your favorite subject? What subject did you dislike?

_____

_____

465. ☐ Did you go home for lunch, take a lunch, or eat lunch at a school cafeteria? What did you usually eat?

_____

_____

_____

466. ☐ Who was at home to greet you when you returned from school?

_____

467. ☐ Was elementary school a happy experience for you? If not, why?

_____

_____

_____

_____

Junior and High School *(Answer Junior and High School separately.)*

468. ☐ Where did you live at this time (town, city, or country)?

_____

_____

469. ☐ Did you attend a public, separate, or private school?

_____

_____

_____

470. ☐ Did you have to wear a uniform?

_____

_____

471. ☐ How far was your school from your home? Did you walk or ride a bus to school?

_____

_____

_____

472. ☐ What did your school look like (large or small; made of brick or wood)?

_____

_____

_____

_____

473. ☐ What did your coatroom and locker look like? Did you tape any pictures in your locker? If so, can you describe them?

_____

_____

_____

_____

474. ☐ Did you wear rubber boots to school?

_____

475. ☐ If female, were you allowed to wear slacks? Do you remember wearing garter belts with long-ribbed stockings? Describe what you wore.

_____

_____

_____

476. ☐ What did a typical classroom look like (desks, blackboards, windows)?

_____

_____

_____

_____

477. ☐ Approximately how many students were in your classes? Were some of the grades combined?

_____

478. ☐ Did you go home for lunch, take a lunch, or eat lunch at school? What would you typically take in your lunch bag?

_____

_____

479. ☐ What were your favorite subjects? Which subjects did you dislike?

_____

_____

_____

480. ☐ Were you an average student, good student, or honors student?

_____

481. ☐ Did you ever go home with a poor report card? If so, what reaction did you get from your parents? Were you rewarded for high marks on your report card?

_____

_____

_____

_____

482. ☐ What was your attitude towards school? Were you ever "sent to the principal's office"? If so, what was your punishment (strap, detention, written apology, lines on the blackboard)?

_____

_____

_____

_____

483. ☐ Did you study hard or cram at the last moment for your exams? Was there a special area in your home where you did homework?

_____

_____

_____

_____

484. ☐ Were you considered popular? Why or why not?

_____

_____

_____

_____

485. ☐ Did you ever win an award (scholastic, athletic)?

_____

_____

_____

486. ☐ Were you involved with the Students' Union committee, school yearbook, or school paper? If so, in what capacity?

_____

_____

_____

_____

487. ☐ Did you play in a school band? If so, what instrument did you play? Were you able to travel to different cities to play in parades? Where?

_____

_____

_____

_____

488. ☐ Were you involved in sports? If so, what sport/s and what position/s?

_____

_____

_____

_____

_____

489. ☐ Were you a cheerleader? If so, what did you wear? Was this a positive experience?

_____

_____

_____

490. ☐ Can you remember any funny incidents that happened in school?

_____

_____

_____

_____

491. ☐ Was there one grade in school that stands out more than the others? Why?

_____

_____

_____

492. ☐ What were your school colors? Was there a school song? If so, can you repeat it?

_____

_____

_____

493. ☐ Do you remember your favorite popular song in high school?

_____

_____

494. ☐ What musical group was famous at that time?

_____

_____

_____

495. ☐ Can you remember getting into fights after school? If so, what happened? Were there bullies you feared?

496. ☐ Did you ever belong to a gang?

497. ☐ Who was at home to greet you when you returned from school?

498. ☐ What did you wear to school? What were the clothing trends? Did you think you were "hip" at that time?

499. ☐ What kind of hairstyle did you wear? Did you color your hair?

500. ☐ Were you a leader or follower throughout your school years?

501. ☐ Who was your best friend throughout school? Name some other friends that you spent time with after school.

502. ☐ Can you think of some slang words from that era?

_____

_____

503. ☐ What did you and your friends do on weekends?

_____

_____

_____

504. ☐ Did you babysit to earn some extra money?

_____

505. ☐ Did you go steady with anyone? Did you ever trade class rings or pins?

_____

506. ☐ Did you have a lot of dates or were you shy around the opposite sex?

_____

507. ☐ Did you take courses by correspondence? Were you home-schooled?

_____

508. ☐ What grade did you complete? Did you graduate from high school? In what year? Did you drop out of school in search of work?

_____

509. ☐ What was said about you in your school yearbook?

_____

_____

510. ☐ With whom did you attend your prom? Was it a happy event? Did you attend an all-night party? Describe that night.

_____

_____

_____

_____

_____

511. ☐ Did you ever have to move to other schools because of divorce, death in the family, or a parent's job? If so, did you find that difficult?

_____

_____

_____

_____

512. ☐ Are some of the friends you had in school still your friends today? Do you see them in person? Name the one student you would love to meet to share memories of those past years.

_____

_____

_____

_____

_____

513. ☐ Did any of your classmates become famous?

_____

514. ☐ Were you sad when high school ended or glad to graduate and go on to university and/or start a career?

_____

_____

515. ☐ Have you ever attended a high school reunion? What happened?

516. ☐ What do you think are some of the differences between going to school then and going to school now?

Post-Secondary Education

517. ☐ Were you the first member of your family to further your education?

518. ☐ Did you go to university? A business school? A trade school? Nursing school?

519. ☐ Did your family expect you to pursue post-secondary education? Was this your goal as well? Which career path did your parents want you to take?

520. ☐ Was your family happy about your educational decisions?

521. ☐ Did you work in order to pay for your tuition, earn a scholarship, receive assistance from your family, or obtain a loan?

522. ☐ Did you live at home or in a dormitory? If in a dormitory, did you have a roommate? What was his or her name? Was it a positive experience? Did you go home for special holidays?

523. ☐ What courses did you major in? What was the best course you ever took?

524. ☐ How would you rate yourself as a student during those years?

525. ☐ Were you mentored by a special teacher or professor?

526. ☐ Were you really organized in the way you studied or did you cram?

527. ☐ Did you study most of the time, or did you have a busy social life?

_____

_____

_____

528. ☐ Were you involved with politics or any other special cause/s?

_____

_____

_____

_____

529. ☐ Did you ever play pranks with friends? If so, what happened?

_____

_____

_____

530. ☐ Were you a member of a sorority or fraternity? Which one?
Describe "rush week".

_____

_____

_____

531. ☐ Were you on any sports teams? If so, describe which ones and what
position/s you held. Was your team a winner in the league?

_____

_____

_____

532. ☐ Was there one specific course or degree that propelled you into
your future career?

_____

533. ☐ What goals did you set during your post-secondary education? Did you reach them? If not, why not?

_____

_____

_____

534. ☐ Did your receive any special honors or awards?

_____

_____

535. ☐ In what year did you graduate? Did you receive a special gift (gold watch, trip, car)?

_____

536. ☐ Did anyone in your graduating class become famous?

_____

537. ☐ Have you kept in touch with your friends from that era? If so, do you get together physically or do you keep in touch via telephone and/or correspondence?

_____

_____

538. ☐ Has there been a class reunion since you left? What year did that occur and what happened?

_____

_____

_____

Memories of Careers

539. ❐ Were there any jobs you took prior to working at your main career? If so, what were they?

_____

_____

_____

_____

_____

540. ❐ What career did you choose? How did your decision come about?

_____

_____

_____

_____

541. ❐ Were/are you a salaried employee or self-employed? Are you a member of a union? Share your thoughts about unions.

_____

_____

_____

_____

542. ❐ Were/are you happy with your initial choice or did you find yourself venturing off to other jobs?

_____

_____

_____

_____

543. ❐ How old were you when you began your career?

_____

_____

544. ❐ Do you remember the amount of your first paycheck?

_____

_____

545. ☐ What were the work hours for your first job? Did you have to do shift work? If so, did the hours have an adverse effect on you?

_____

_____

_____

_____

546. ☐ Describe the responsibilities of your career/s over the years.

_____

_____

_____

_____

547. ☐ Did you receive promotions and/or raises over the course of your career? Describe what happened.

_____

_____

_____

548. ☐ Could you have gone as far as you did in your career without your education? Why or why not?

_____

_____

_____

549. ☐ Was there a particular accomplishment at work that you felt very proud of? If so, describe what happened.

_____

_____

_____

550. ☐ Did/do you feel stressed or enjoy the challenge of your position/s?

551. ☐ Did/do you have to travel? Did/does the travelling present problems?

552. ☐ Was/is this job one that you didn't/don't enjoy but stay/ed on in order to earn a living?

553. ☐ Were you ever fired or laid off? If so, was this a big emotional set-back? What action did you take to get yourself back to work? What lesson did you learn from this unfortunate happening?

554. ☐ Were you ever employed within a family business? Was this a satisfactory arrangement or did conflict arise?

555. ❑ Did you ever live or work in a culture that was far away from your homeland? If so, where? Did you enjoy this experience?

556. ❑ Did/does your home life ever suffer because of career demands?

557. ❑ Did/do you get along well with your boss/es? If not, why not?

558. ❑ If female, did you stay at home after having children? Was/is the adjustment difficult for you?

Memories of
the Military

559. ☐ What made you decide to join the military? Were you drafted or was it a personal choice?

_____

_____

_____

_____

560. ☐ Were you concerned about the world situation at that time?

_____

_____

_____

561. ☐ Were other family members also in the military when you joined?

_____

_____

562. ☐ Where were you living when you joined the service?

_____

_____

563. ☐ What branch did you join?

_____

_____

564. ☐ Where did you undergo your basic training? Was it tough?

_____

_____

_____

_____

565. ☐ What was your area of expertise in the military?

_____

_____

_____

_____

566. ☐ What rank did you hold?

567. ☐ What did your uniform look like?

568. ☐ What duties were required of you?

569. ☐ Did you study while in the service? If so, what did you study?

570. ☐ Where were you stationed while in the military?

571. ☐ Were you required to move your family often over the years?

572. ☐ Did you ever wish you had continued on with post-secondary education as opposed to joining the military?

573. ☐ When was your first introduction to war?

574. ☐ Were you ever in combat? Were you wounded? Did you kill anyone? If so, how did this affect you?

575. ☐ Were care packages and letters of major importance for morale?

576. ☐ Were you awarded any medal during your service? If so, why? Where is the medal kept now? Is this medal to be bequeathed to someone special?

577. ☐ Are memories of the war still in your thoughts on a regular basis? What do you think about?

_____

_____

_____

_____

578. ☐ Are there any war songs that are special to you?

_____

_____

_____

579. ☐ Do you still keep in touch with your war buddies?

_____

_____

_____

_____

580. ☐ Did a member of your family die in a war?

_____

_____

_____

_____

581. ☐ How many years were you in the service before returning to civilian life?

_____

_____

_____

582. ☐ When you left the service, where did you locate and what career did you pursue?

_____

_____

_____

_____

583. ☐ What did serving in the military mean to you?

_____

_____

_____

_____

584. ☐ Looking back, did your military service have a profound effect on your life? Describe your feelings.

_____

_____

_____

_____

Memories of Parents

Your Mother

585. ☐ What was/is your mother's full name (including her maiden name)?

_____

_____

586. ☐ Where was your mother born? In what year was she born?

_____

_____

587. ☐ Where was your mother raised as a child?

_____

_____

588. ☐ Describe your mother's physical characteristics (height, weight, eye color, hair color, build).

_____

_____

_____

_____

_____

589. ☐ How did your mother dress while you were growing up?

_____

_____

_____

_____

590. ☐ Was/is your mother an extrovert or an introvert?

_____

_____

_____

591. ☐ Was/is your mother a kind and caring person, often doing for others?

_____

_____

_____

_____

592. ☐ Was/is your mother a good mother and did/does her family always come first?

_____

_____

_____

_____

593. ☐ What qualities did/does your mother have that made/make you very proud?

_____

_____

_____

_____

594. ☐ What is the happiest memory you have of your mother?

_____

_____

_____

_____

595. ☐ Do you feel that you are very similar to your mother?

_____

_____

596. ☐ Describe your relationship with your mother.

_____

_____

_____

_____

597. ☐ Was your mother a strict disciplinarian or did she leave the disciplining to your father? How were you disciplined?

_____

_____

_____

598. ☐ Describe the negative side of your mother, if there was/is one.

_____

_____

_____

_____

599. ☐ Was/is your mother emotional? Have you ever seen her cry?

_____

_____

_____

_____

600. ☐ Was/is it usual for your mother to talk often about the past or was/is she always looking ahead to the future?

_____

_____

_____

601. ☐ How did your mother deal with stress while you were growing up?

_____

_____

_____

_____

_____

602. ☐ Do you know if your mother had to endure any traumatic situations as a child or in her marriage? Describe them.

_____

_____

_____

_____

603. ☐ Was/is your mother in good health and has she been for most of her life? If not, describe her health problems. What effect did this have on the family?

_____

_____

_____

_____

_____

604. ☐ Did you inherit any health problems from your mother?

_____

_____

_____

_____

605. ☐ What was/is your mother's religious affiliation? Was/is she involved with her church on a regular basis? How did/does her faith affect the family?

606. ☐ Was/is your mother open or inhibited about sex?

607. ☐ What level of education did your mother obtain?

608. ☐ Did your mother work in a salaried position? Was it from necessity or because she wanted a career?

609. ☐ Did/does your mother enjoy housework?

610. ☐ Was/is your mother a good cook? Did/does she entertain at home?

611. ☐ Was there a favorite recipe of your mother's that you remember from your childhood?

_____

_____

_____

_____

612. ☐ What were/are your mother's favorite hobbies? Describe them.

_____

_____

_____

613. ☐ Describe any special skills or talents your mother had/has.

_____

_____

_____

_____

614. ☐ In your opinion, did/does your mother think life was/is a struggle? Why or why not?

_____

_____

_____

_____

615. ☐ Are you aware of disappointments that your mother experienced?

_____

_____

_____

_____

616. ☐ How would you describe your mother's social status in the community?

_____

_____

_____

_____

617. ☐ Was/is your mother close to her sibling/s? Describe their relationship.

_____

_____

_____

_____

618. ☐ Did/does your mother have a favorite sibling?

_____

_____

619. ☐ Was/is there a sibling who was/is considered a "troublemaker"?

_____

_____

_____

_____

620. ☐ Did/does your mother spend a lot of time with her siblings?

_____

_____

_____

_____

621. ☐ Was/is your mother involved in the community? In politics?

_____

_____

_____

_____

622. ☐ Did/does your mother play a musical instrument? If so, which one? Did this musical talent become a profession?

_____

_____

_____

_____

623. ☐ Was/is your mother an active participant in sports or an observer?

_____

_____

_____

_____

624. ☐ If your mother is deceased, when and how did she die?

_____

_____

_____

625. ☐ Where are your mother's remains (in which city and at what cemetery)? Is there a special time you visit the cemetery?

_____

_____

_____

_____

626. ☐ Did/do you have difficulty accepting her death?

_____

_____

_____

_____

627. ☐ Do you have any regrets about "unfinished business" with your mother?

_____

_____

_____

_____

_____

628. ☐ Did you receive a keepsake from your mother before or after her death that you treasure?

_____

_____

629. ☐ Looking back, what was the most important thing you learned from your mother?

_____

_____

_____

_____

Your Father

630. ☐ What was/is your father's full name?

_____

631. ☐ Where was your father born? In what year was he born?

_____

632. ☐ Where was your father raised as a child?

_____

_____

633. ☐ Describe your father's physical characteristics (height, weight, eye color, hair color, build).

634. ☐ How did your father dress while you were growing up?

635. ☐ Was/is your father an extrovert or an introvert?

636. ☐ Was/is your father a kind and caring person, often doing for others?

637. ☐ Was/is your father a good father and did/does his family always come first?

638. ☐ What qualities did/does your father have that made/make you very proud?

_____

_____

_____

_____

639. ☐ What was/is the happiest memory you have of your father?

_____

_____

_____

_____

640. ☐ Do you feel that you are very similar to your father?

_____

_____

_____

_____

641. ☐ Describe your relationship with your father.

_____

_____

_____

_____

642. ☐ Was your father a strict disciplinarian or did he leave the disciplining to your mother?

_____

_____

643. ☐ Describe the negative side of your father, if there was/is one.

_____

_____

_____

_____

644. ☐ Was/is your father emotional? Have you ever seen him cry?

_____

_____

_____

645. ☐ Was/is it usual for your father to talk often about the past or was/is he always looking ahead to the future?

_____

_____

_____

646. ☐ How did your father deal with stress while you were growing up?

_____

_____

_____

_____

647. ☐ Do you know if your father had to endure any traumatic situations as a child or in his marriage?

_____

_____

_____

_____

648. ☐ Was/is your father in good health and has he been for most of his life? If not, describe his health problems. What effect did this have on the family?

649. ☐ Did you inherit any health problems from your father?

650. ☐ What was/is your father's religious affiliation? Was/is he involved with his church on a regular basis? How did/does his faith affect the family?

651. ☐ Was/is your father open or inhibited about sex?

652. ☐ What level of education did your father obtain?

653. ☐ What was/is your father's occupation?

_____

_____

_____

654. ☐ If retired, did he stay with the same company until retirement?

_____

_____

_____

655. ☐ Did/does your father handle all the financial affairs of the family?

_____

_____

_____

656. ☐ Did/does your father ever discuss the work he did as a child or young man? If so, describe his employment.

_____

_____

_____

_____

657. ☐ In your opinion, did/does your father think life was/is a struggle? Why or why not?

_____

_____

_____

_____

658. ☐ Are you aware of disappointments that your father experienced?

659. ☐ How would you describe your father's social status in the community?

660. ☐ Was your father actively involved in politics? If so, how did this come about and what party did he support?

661. ☐ Describe special skills or talents your father had/has.

127

662. ☐ Did/does your father play a musical instrument? If so, which one? Did this musical talent become a profession?

_____

_____

_____

_____

_____

663. ☐ Was/is your father a handyman? If so, what did/does he do?

_____

_____

_____

_____

664. ☐ Did/does he have any hobbies? Describe them.

_____

_____

_____

_____

665. ☐ Did/does your father like to fish and/or hunt? If so, what stories have you heard?

_____

_____

_____

_____

666. ☐ Did/does your father watch a lot of television?

_____

_____

667. ☐ Was/is your father an active participant in sports or an observer?

_____
_____
_____
_____

668. ☐ Which sports were/are his favorites?

_____
_____

669. ☐ Was/is your father close to his siblings? Describe their relationships.

_____
_____
_____
_____

670. ☐ Did/does your father spend a lot of time with his siblings?

_____
_____
_____

671. ☐ Did/does your father have a favorite sibling?

_____

672. ☐ Was/is there a sibling who was/is considered a "troublemaker"?

_____
_____
_____

673. ☐ If your father is deceased, when and how did he die?

674. ☐ Did/do you have difficulty accepting his death?

675. ☐ Do you have any regrets about "unfinished business" with your father?

676. ☐ Did you receive a keepsake from your father before or after his death that you treasure?

677. ☐ Where are your father's remains (in which city and at what cemetery)? Is there a special time when you visit the cemetery?

678. ☐ Looking back, what was the most important thing you learned from your father?

_____

_____

_____

_____

General Questions

679. ☐ Were you raised by your parents or someone else?

_____

_____

_____

_____

680. ☐ What did you call your parents?

_____

681. ☐ Was more than one language spoken in your home?

_____

682. ☐ Do you know how your parents met? If so, tell about their courtship.

_____

_____

_____

_____

683. ☐ How old was each of your parents when they married?

_____

_____

_____

684. ☐ What do you know about their wedding (when, where, big or small)?

_____

_____

_____

_____

685. ☐ Where did your parents live when they first married (in the country, in the city; in a house or in an apartment)?

_____

_____

_____

_____

686. ☐ Do you know how much your parents' first home cost?

_____

687. ☐ Can you describe your mother and father's relationship (formal, loving, indifferent, strained, ambivalent)?

_____

_____

_____

_____

688. ☐ In general, would you describe your parents' marriage as a happy one? Why or why not?

_____

_____

_____

_____

689. ☐ Were/are there things that your mother and/or father did/do that upset you? Did/do you vow not to repeat their mistakes in your life?

690. ☐ Did your parents experience any major hardships (health problems, financial setbacks, addictions, unemployment, divorce, death)? If so, how was the family affected?

691. ☐ What issues were your parents strict about while you were growing up? Were they stricter than most other parents?

692. ☐ Are there special stories your parents shared with you that you recall?

Parents

693. ☐ Were/are you able to spend a lot of time with your parents? If so, what were/are some of the things you did/do? If not, why?

_____

_____

_____

_____

_____

694. ☐ How did you and your parents spend vacations (where, when, and with whom)?

_____

_____

_____

_____

_____

695. ☐ How did/do your parents utilize their free time (for example, gardening, games, movies, sports, and/or hobbies)?

_____

_____

_____

_____

_____

696. ☐ Did/do your parents socialize often? Who are their friends?

_____

_____

_____

_____

697. ☐ Did/do your parents like to dance?

_____

_____

698. ☐ What mode of transportation did/do they usually use to travel?

_____

_____

699. ☐ What were/are your parents like as grandparents?

_____

_____

_____

_____

_____

700. ☐ Upon reflection, do you think your parents lived a fulfilling life?

_____

_____

_____

_____

_____

701. ☐ When you reminisce about your mother and father, do you feel you understand them more now that you have matured?

_____

_____

_____

_____

Memories of Grandparents

Grandmother on Mother's Side

702. ☐ What was/is your grandmother's full name (including her maiden name)?

_____

_____

703. ☐ What was/is your grandmother's birth date? Where was your grandmother born (city, town, country)?

_____

_____

_____

_____

704. ☐ Where did your grandmother grow up (city, town, country)?

_____

_____

705. ☐ What did/do you call your grandmother?

_____

_____

706. ☐ What did/does your grandmother look like?

_____

_____

_____

_____

707. ☐ Was/is there a physical characteristic of your grandmother that you will always remember?

_____

_____

_____

_____

708. ☐ Do you have a picture in your mind of what your grandmother usually wore/wears? If so, describe her.

_____

_____

_____

_____

_____

709. ☐ Was/is your grandmother a quiet or outgoing lady?

_____

_____

_____

_____

710. ☐ Was/is your grandmother indulgent or strict with you?

_____

_____

_____

711. ☐ Did/does your grandmother have a sense of humor?

_____

_____

_____

712. ☐ Was/is your grandmother an optimist or a pessimist? Did/do you look forward to your visits with her?

_____

_____

_____

713. ☐ Did your grandmother work outside the home? If so, what was her occupation?

_____

_____

_____

714. ☐ Did/does your grandmother have special skills that impressed you?

_____

_____

_____

_____

715. ☐ Do you remember your grandmother as being in good health or sick much of the time?

_____

_____

_____

716. ☐ Can you describe something special you remember about your grandmother (something she said, something she did)?

_____

_____

_____

_____

Grandfather on Mother's Side

717. ☐ What was/is your grandfather's full name?

718. ☐ What was/is your grandfather's birth date? Where was your grandfather born (city, town, country)?

719. ☐ Where did your grandfather grow up (city, town, country)?

720. ☐ What did/do you call your grandfather?

721. ☐ What did/does your grandfather look like?

722. ☐ Was/is there a physical characteristic of your grandfather that you will always remember?

723. ❐ Do you have a picture in your mind of what your grandfather usually wore/wears? If so, describe him.

_____

_____

_____

_____

_____

724. ❐ Was/is your grandfather a quiet or "take charge" person?

_____

_____

725. ❐ Was/is your grandfather indulgent or strict with you?

_____

_____

_____

_____

726. ❐ Did/does your grandfather have a sense of humor?

_____

_____

_____

_____

727. ❐ Was/is your grandfather an optimist or a pessimist? Did/do you look forward to your visits with him?

_____

_____

_____

_____

728. ☐ What did/does your grandfather do for a living? If he is retired or deceased, did he work at one job all of his life?

_____

_____

_____

_____

_____

729. ☐ Did/does your grandfather have special skills that you admire?

_____

_____

_____

_____

730. ☐ Do you remember your grandfather as being in good health or sick much of the time?

_____

_____

_____

_____

731. ☐ Can you describe something special you remember about your grandfather (something he said, something he did)?

_____

_____

_____

_____

General Questions about Your Mother's Grandparents

732. ☐ Did your grandparents immigrate from another country? Which one? Why? When? How? Where?

_____

_____

_____

_____

733. ☐ Did they tell you stories about their early lives? If so, describe some of their experiences.

_____

_____

_____

_____

734. ☐ Did your grandparents live through the Depression? Did they share any interesting stories with you that you'd like to relate?

_____

_____

_____

_____

735. ☐ Did you ever hear about your grandparents' courtship? How long did they go together and how old were they when they married?

_____

_____

_____

_____

736. ☐ How many children did/do your grandparents have?

_____

_____

_____

_____

737. ☐ If deceased, how many years were your grandparents married? If still alive, how many years have they been married? Were they ever married to someone else? If so, what happened?

_____

_____

_____

_____

738. ☐ Did/do your parents get along well with your grandparents? Did/do your grandparents live nearby?

_____

_____

_____

_____

739. ☐ What influence did/do your grandparents have on you? Did/do they play a prominent role in your life?

_____

_____

_____

_____

_____

740. ☐ Were/are you closest to your grandmother or your grandfather? Why is this relationship special?

_____

_____

_____

_____

741. ☐ If your grandparents are deceased, tell when and how they died.

_____

_____

_____

_____

742. ☐ If deceased, where are they buried (place, cemetery)? Do you ever visit their graves? If so, how often?

_____

_____

_____

Answer questions 702 to 742 regarding your grandparents on your father's side. This is the time for you to use your journal or notebook.

Memories of Siblings

Answer questions 743 to 757 for each sister and/or brother.
This is the time for you to use your journal or notebook.

743. ☐ If you were an only child, describe what it was like being one.

_____

_____

_____

_____

_____

744. ☐ What was/is your brother/sister's full name?

_____

_____

745. ☐ What was/is your brother/sister's birth date? Where was he/she
born (city, town, country)?

_____

_____

_____

746. ☐ Did/do you have a nickname for your brother/sister?

_____

_____

747. ☐ What did/does he/she look like (height; build; eye color; hair: color,
straight or curly, thin or thick)?

_____

_____

_____

_____

748. ☐ Describe his/her personality (outgoing, shy, optimistic, pessimistic).

_____

_____

_____

_____

749. ☐ Did/do you get along with this brother/sister? If not, what caused the problems? Are you now close to each other or have you become emotionally distant?

_____

_____

_____

_____

750. ☐ What did/do you like about this brother/sister? Is there anything you dislike?

_____

_____

_____

_____

751. ☐ Did you feel that your parents favored this brother/sister? If so, why?

_____

_____

_____

_____

752. ☐ Was there a special skill this brother/sister had that made you proud?

_____
_____
_____
_____

753. ☐ Do you think you were competitive with him/her?

_____
_____
_____

754. ☐ As far as you know, has this brother/sister had a rewarding life? Why or why not?

_____
_____
_____

755. ☐ What paths did he/she take after leaving home?

_____
_____
_____
_____

756. ☐ Was/is he/she different as an adult from what he/she was as a child? If so, what happened?

_____
_____
_____
_____

757. ☐ Was this sibling adopted? If so, how would you describe his/her adjustment to your family? Did you feel he/she wanted to search for his/her biological family?

_____

_____

_____

_____

_____

_____

_____

Memories of Extended Family

Aunts and Uncles

Answer questions 758 to 765 for each aunt and uncle. This is the time for you to use your journal or notebook.

Mother's Side

758. ☐ What was/is your uncle/aunt's full name?

_____

_____

759. ☐ What was/is your uncle/aunt's birth date? Where was he/she born (city, town, country)?

_____

_____

_____

760. ☐ What did/does this uncle/aunt look like (height; build; eye color; hair: color, straight or curly, thin or thick)?

_____

_____

_____

_____

_____

761. ☐ Describe this uncle/aunt's personality (outgoing, shy, optimistic, pessimistic).

_____

_____

_____

_____

Extended Family

762. ☐ Was/is this uncle/aunt one of your favorites? What was/is so special about this person?

_____

_____

_____

763. ☐ Did/do you spend a lot of time with this uncle/aunt? If not, why not?

_____

_____

_____

764. ☐ Did/do your parents get along with this uncle/aunt? If not, why not?

_____

_____

_____

765. ☐ If this uncle/aunt is deceased, what was the cause of death?

_____

_____

_____

For each aunt and uncle, you may wish to name their children and relate your experiences with your cousins. This is the time for you to use your journal or notebook.

Father's Side

Answer questions 758 to 765 for each aunt and uncle.

Step-Family

Any or all of the questions in the Parents and Siblings sections can be used to record step-family memories. Use your journal or notebook for this purpose.

766. ☐ Was/is your step-family structure sound or was/is being in a step-family situation difficult for you? Describe the joys and/or difficulties experienced by your blended family and what effect this has had on your life.

_____

_____

_____

_____

_____

Memories of Courtship and Marriage

Courtship/Dating

767. ☐ What were the circumstances of your first meeting with your mate?

_____

_____

_____

_____

768. ☐ Who pursued whom?

_____

769. ☐ What attracted you to your mate? Was it "love at first sight"?

_____

_____

_____

_____

770. ☐ How old was each of you when you first met?

_____

_____

771. ☐ What did you do on your first date?

_____

_____

_____

772. ☐ Describe your mate's physical appearance during courtship. Was his/her appearance the main reason you first connected?

_____

_____

_____

773. ☐ Did you consider him/her to have a great personality? What did he/she say or do that impressed you?

_____

_____

_____

_____

774. ☐ Describe your first kiss (when, where, what was it like)?

_____

_____

_____

775. ☐ What were the rules for courting in your day? Did you have a chaperone?

_____

_____

_____

776. ☐ Was there a dating curfew imposed by your parents? What time did you have to be home on weekdays? On the weekends?

_____

_____

777. ☐ Describe some of the places you went or some of the things you did on dates (for example, box socials, dances, movies, beach parties).

_____

_____

_____

_____

778. ☐ Did you have special pet names for each other? If so, what were they?

_____

_____

_____

779. ☐ Did you and your mate have a favorite song? If so, what was it? When you hear that song now, do you get sentimental?

_____

_____

_____

780. ☐ Were you ever jealous during your courtship? If so, what happened?

_____

_____

_____

_____

781. ☐ Did you quarrel often or break up for a time? Were those quarrels a symptom that you should have paid more attention to and maybe not ventured into marriage?

_____

_____

_____

_____

782. ☐ Looking back, do you think you were mature enough to have made a commitment to marry?

_____

_____

_____

Engagement

783. ☐ How long did you know each other before the marriage proposal?

784. ☐ Describe the marriage proposal (when, where, how)?

785 ☐ What was your parents' reaction when you told them you were getting married? Did you ask their permission and receive their blessing?

786. ☐ How did you celebrate your engagement?

787. ☐ Did your bridesmaids have any showers for you? If so, how many and what kind of showers were they? What was your favorite present? Did you have a trousseau tea?

The Wedding

788. ☐ How old was each of you when you married?

789. ☐ What day, month, and year were you married? Where were you married (city, town, country)?

790. ☐ Were you married in a church or did you have a civil ceremony? Who officiated at your wedding?

791. ☐ Who were your attendants? What did they wear? Are you still in touch with any of your attendants?

792. ☐ What did you and your mate wear on your wedding day (formal or informal)? Did the bride wear her mother's dress?

793. ☐ Describe what your wedding rings looked like.

_____

_____

_____

794. ☐ Was it a large wedding? How many guests were there? Did you do most of the planning yourself or did your parents help?

_____

_____

_____

_____

795. ☐ Did your parents help to pay for the wedding, were the costs shared, or did you assume the entire responsibility?

_____

_____

_____

_____

796. ☐ What was the weather like on your wedding day?

_____

_____

797. ☐ Describe what your feelings were on your wedding day. Were you both nervous?

_____

_____

_____

_____

798. ☐ Who walked the bride down the aisle? Was that moment special?

_____

_____

_____

_____

799. ☐ Did everything proceed as planned throughout the day? Describe what happened if problems occurred.

_____

_____

_____

_____

_____

800. ☐ Describe your wedding decorations and cake. Did a family member make the cake?

_____

_____

_____

_____

801. ☐ Where was your reception held? What kind of food was prepared? Who was the master of ceremonies? Describe your reception.

_____

_____

_____

_____

802. ☐ Did you have a professional photographer? Were you pleased with the pictures? Do you ever reminisce by bringing out the pictures?

_____

_____

_____

_____

803. ☐ What do you remember most about your wedding day? Where did you spend your wedding night? Was it a good choice?

_____

_____

_____

_____

The Honeymoon

804. ☐ Did you have a honeymoon? If so, where did you go and for how long? Were you pleased with your choice of destination?

_____

_____

_____

_____

805. ☐ If you went away, did the weather cooperate? If not, describe what happened. Did this mar your plans?

_____

_____

_____

_____

806. ☐ Was your honeymoon a gift from your family? Looking back, do you wish you had eloped? If so, why?

_____

_____

_____

_____

Married Life

807. ☐ How many in-laws did you acquire?

_____

_____

808. ☐ How was/is your relationship with your mother-in-law and/or father-in-law?

_____

_____

_____

_____

_____

809. ☐ Where did you live when you were first married? For how long?

_____

_____

_____

810. ☐ How much did your first home/apartment cost per month?

_____

_____

811. ☐ Describe your first home/apartment (inside and outside).

_____

_____

_____

_____

812. ☐ Did you both work during your marriage? Did this present any problems?

_____

_____

_____

_____

813. ☐ As a couple, were you thrifty or did you live beyond your means?

_____

_____

_____

_____

814. ☐ When you were first married, what was your monthly food bill?

_____

815. ☐ What joys did you experience during the early years of marriage?

_____

_____

_____

_____

816. ☐ What hardships, if any, did you experience during the early years of marriage?

_____

_____

_____

_____

817. ☐ What did you discover was the biggest adjustment in living together as a couple?

818. ☐ Was your lifestyle altered dramatically after you married? Why or why not?

819. ☐ What did you find out about your spouse once you were married that you didn't know about before?

820. ☐ What strengths did/do you both contribute to the marriage?

Current Questions

821. ☐ What outstanding characteristics would you say apply to your mate?

_____

_____

_____

_____

_____

822. ☐ Are/were you and your mate alike? If not, what are/were your differences?

_____

_____

_____

_____

_____

823. ☐ How often do/did you and your mate go out socially? What is/was your favorite activity?

_____

_____

_____

_____

_____

824. ☐ Does/did your mate surprise you with gifts, love notes, flowers, phone calls, or other tokens of affection?

_____

_____

_____

_____

825. ☐ What was the most memorable gift you ever received from your mate?

_____

_____

_____

_____

826. ☐ What was the most memorable gift you ever gave your mate?

_____

_____

_____

_____

827. ☐ Was there one romantic occasion that you cherish?

_____

_____

_____

_____

828. ☐ Do/did you always try to look your best for your mate?

_____

_____

829. ☐ Can you think of something humorous about your mate? Is a sense of humor important to you in a marriage?

_____

_____

_____

_____

830. ☐ Do/did you and your mate share chores? If not, why not?

_____

_____

_____

_____

831. ☐ Do/did you and your mate do volunteer work within the
community?

_____

_____

_____

_____

832. ☐ At what point in your marriage were you the happiest? Why?

_____

_____

_____

_____

_____

833. ☐ Are/were there problems pertaining to alcoholism, gambling,
abuse, or finances? Did these issues contribute to a divorce or were
they resolved? What effect has this had on your marriage?

_____

_____

_____

_____

_____

834. ☐ What qualities would you choose in a mate now, if you had to do it all over again?

_____

_____

_____

_____

835. ☐ What would you do if you and/or your mate won $10 million?

_____

_____

_____

_____

836. ☐ If your mate has died, at what age did he/she die and what was the cause?

_____

_____

_____

_____

837. ☐ Where is your mate buried (city, town, country; name of cemetery)?

_____

_____

838. ☐ How did his/her death affect your life?

_____

_____

_____

_____

839. ☐ Did you divorce your mate or did he/she divorce you? Why?

840. ☐ Was the divorce a jolting experience for you? Describe what happened.

841. ☐ How many years were you married before you divorced? Did you try counselling before making the final decision?

842. ☐ How did your family react to the divorce? Did you remain in contact with your in-laws?

843. ☐ Were your friends supportive or did they desert you?

_____

_____

_____

_____

844. ☐ Did you remain in your home after the divorce? If not, what happened?

_____

_____

_____

845. ☐ What would you say was the greatest lesson from your divorce?

_____

_____

_____

_____

In cases of remarriage or common-law, answer questions 846 to 853.

846. ☐ Name your spouse/s.

_____

_____

847. ☐ If you are living or lived common-law, why did you make this choice?

_____

_____

_____

_____

848. ☐ How did you meet this mate?

_____

_____

_____

_____

_____

849. ☐ When and where were you married the second time? Other times?

_____

_____

_____

850. ☐ Did you have any children with this spouse? If so, you can answer any of the questions in the 'Memories of Parenting' section.

_____

_____

_____

851. ☐ Were there any conflicts in raising natural and/or step-children? If so, how were these issues resolved?

_____

_____

_____

_____

852. ☐ Would you consider this marriage a success or a stressful time?

_____

_____

_____

_____

_____

853. ☐   Would you recommend a blended family to others considering such a choice? Why or why not?

_____

_____

_____

_____

_____

You may use any of the questions from the Courtship and Marriage section if they relate to additional marriages.

Memories of Parenting

Although many of the questions in this section are addressed to mothers, they can also be answered by fathers. Simply change "you" to "your wife" where this is appropriate.

854. ☐ Did you and your mate discuss having children before you married?

855. ☐ If you were an only child, were you determined to have more than one child of your own? Why?

856. ☐ How soon did you have your first child after you were married?

857. ☐ Did you ever suffer a miscarriage? More than one? How did you deal with such a trauma? Do you still talk about that child?

858. ☐ Did you ever have an abortion? If so, do you still think it was the best decision for you at that time? Describe your feelings.

859. ☐ Did you ever lose a child to SIDS? How did you cope?

_____

_____

_____

_____

860. ☐ Were you ever faced with the problem of infertility? If so, did you try in-vitro fertilization? Was it successful?

_____

_____

_____

_____

Answer questions 861 to 891 for each child. This is the time for you to use your journal or notebook.

Infancy

861. ☐ Where and how did you tell your husband that you were pregnant? What was his reaction? Was this birth planned?

_____

_____

_____

_____

862. ☐ What is the full name of this son/daughter? How did you choose this child's name? Was he/she named after a family member?

_____

_____

_____

_____

863. How old were you and your mate when this child was born?

864. What is your son's/daughter's birth date? Where was he/she born (city, town, country)?

865. Did you have a difficult pregnancy? Did you suffer from morning sickness? What cravings did you develop? How many pounds did you gain? Did they disappear easily after the birth?

866. Describe your trip to the hospital to have this baby.

867. How many hours were you in labor? Did you have a natural birth? Did you experience complications?

868. ❏ Who was the first person you called after the birth?

869. ❏ How long was your hospital stay? Did you have help when you came home from the hospital? If so, who helped you?

870. ❏ Were you able to nurse your child or did you bottle feed? Was this a positive experience?

871. ❏ What did this child look like? Did he/she have a happy disposition? Did he/she have any sleep problems?

872. ❏ Were both you and your mate involved in taking care of him/her?

873. ▢ Was Dr. Spock your "Bible" in raising children? If not, did you have help from family or friends or do most things by instinct?

_____

_____

_____

_____

874. ▢ Did you or anyone else make anything special for this child (for example, knitting, needlepoint, wooden toy, decoration).

_____

_____

_____

_____

875. ▢ What did this child's nursery look like?

_____

_____

_____

_____

876. ▢ Did this child have good eating habits or was it a challenge to get him/her to eat properly?

_____

_____

_____

_____

877. ▢ At what age did he/she walk? At what age was he/she toilet trained?

_____

878. ☐ Was he/she healthy most of the time or sick a lot of the time?

_____

_____

_____

879. ☐ Did you ever have to rush him/her to the hospital? If so, why?

_____

_____

_____

_____

880. ☐ Were you diligent in filling out a baby book and taking pictures?

_____

_____

Later Years

881. ☐ What does he/she look like (height; build; eye color; hair: color, straight or curly, thin or thick)?

_____

_____

_____

_____

882. ☐ Describe his/her personality (outgoing, shy, optimistic, pessimistic)?

_____

_____

_____

_____

883. ☐ Was he/she a quiet or an active child?

884. ☐ What do you think is his/her best character trait?

885. ☐ Did he/she belong to any clubs, participate in sports, and/or take music lessons?

886. ☐ Was he/she a good student?

887. ☐ Was he/she difficult as a teenager? If so, what specific problems did you encounter?

888. ☐ Was there some special gift you received from him/her that you treasure? What is it?

889. ☐ Describe some of the special times you had with him/her.

_____

_____

_____

_____

890. ☐ How did you feel when he/she left home?

_____

_____

_____

891. ☐ What did this child do after leaving home? Were you in agreement with his/her choice? If not, why not?

_____

_____

_____

_____

General

892. ☐ How much an hour did you have to pay a babysitter?

_____

_____

893. ☐ Did you have a nanny? If so, do you now feel that was a good choice? Why or why not?

_____

_____

_____

_____

894. ☐ How did your children get along with each other?

_____

_____

_____

_____

895. ☐ Were your ideas about child rearing different from the way you were raised? If so, in what way were they different?

_____

_____

_____

_____

896. ☐ How did you discipline your children? Do you believe in spanking?

_____

_____

_____

_____

897. ☐ Were you considered strict or permissive as a parent?

_____

_____

898. ☐ What rules were the toughest to enforce with your children?

_____

_____

_____

_____

899. ☐ Did you and your mate both work while raising your children?

900. ☐ Were you ever a single parent? If so, describe some of the challenges you faced.

901. ☐ Did you make time for yourself, regardless of your responsibilities as a parent?

902. ☐ What traditions did/do you enjoy the most with your children?

903. ☐ Do you consider that you were a good parent? What was the hardest part of parenting?

904. ☐ Did having children prove to be a very rewarding experience? If
        not, what do you think happened?

        _____

        _____

        _____

        _____

        _____

905. ☐ What values did you instill in your children?

        _____

        _____

        _____

        _____

906. ☐ If you had to parent your children again, would you do anything
        differently?

        _____

        _____

        _____

        _____

        _____

907. ☐ Do you think boys or girls are easier to raise, and why do you feel
        that way?

        _____

        _____

        _____

        _____

908. ☐   When the last child left home, was it a difficult time for you?

_____

_____

_____

_____

909. ☐   How did your life change after your children left?

_____

_____

_____

_____

910. ☐   What is your opinion of the current trend of children moving back home with their parents? Would you allow this to happen?

_____

_____

_____

_____

911. ☐   When you assess your own parenting skills, how good a job do you think your parents did in raising you?

_____

_____

If you wish, you can list the names of your children, their mates, and wedding dates. Also mention if any children decided to remain single. This is the time to use your journal or notebook.

Memories of Grandparenting

912. ☐ Do you remember where you were when you were told you were going to become a grandparent for the very first time?

_____

_____

_____

_____

913. ☐ Where were you when your first grandchild was born?

_____

_____

_____

914. ☐ How many grandchildren do you have at this time?

_____

_____

_____

_____

Answer questions 915 to 928 for each grandchild; use your journal or notebook.

915. ☐ What is the full name of this grandson/granddaughter? Was he/she named after a family member? Who are his/her parents?

_____

_____

_____

916. ☐ What is your grandson's/granddaughter's birth date? Where was he/she born (city, town, country)?

_____

_____

917. ☐ Did you help your daughter or daughter-in-law when she returned home from the hospital?

_____

_____

_____

_____

918. ☐ What did you give the baby for a birth gift?

_____

919. ☐ Have you ever hand-made anything special for this grandchild?

_____

_____

_____

920. ☐ Did he/she look like his/her parent did as a baby?

_____

_____

_____

921. ☐ What does your grandchild call you?

_____

922. ☐ Did you babysit for this grandchild when he/she was young? Was this out of necessity or strictly for pleasure?

_____

_____

_____

923. ☐ What treats did you have for him/her when he/she visited?

_____

_____

924. ☐ What activities did you like to do with him/her (for example, reading, sports, playing games)?

_____

_____

_____

_____

_____

925. ☐ Describe his/her personality.

_____

_____

_____

_____

_____

926. ☐ Can you recall one memorable time spent with him/her?

_____

_____

_____

_____

927. ☐ Do you share parts of your past with this child?

_____

_____

_____

_____

928. ☐   Is there a special gift you treasure from this grandchild?

_____

_____

_____

_____

General

929. ☐   Do you miss having babies of your own?

_____

_____

930. ☐   Do you tend to spoil your grandchildren?

_____

_____

_____

931. ☐   If your grandchildren live far away, how often do you see them?

_____

_____

_____

_____

_____

932. ☐   Do any of your grandchildren spend the night with you?

_____

_____

933. ☐ When they visit, how do you feel after they leave?

_____

_____

_____

_____

934. ☐ Do you try to tell your children how they should raise your grandchildren?

_____

_____

_____

935. ☐ How would you describe the way your grandchildren are being raised compared to the way you raised your own children?

_____

_____

_____

_____

936. ☐ How is family life different for your grandchildren from what it was for your own children?

_____

_____

_____

_____

_____

937. ☐ Do you think your grandchildren's value system is different from your value system?

_____

_____

_____

_____

_____

938. ☐ What effect do you feel television has had on your grandchildren?

_____

_____

_____

_____

939. ☐ Do you get frustrated if you see one of your grandchildren taking everything for granted or wanting everything to go his/her way?

_____

_____

_____

_____

940. ☐ Would you want to be their age again? Why or why not?

_____

_____

_____

_____

_____

941. ☐ What is the best thing about being a grandparent? The worst?

_____

_____

_____

_____

942. ☐ What do you want your grandchildren to remember about you?

_____

_____

_____

_____

943. ☐ What do you think you have taught your grandchildren?

_____

_____

_____

_____

944. ☐ What have your grandchildren added to your life?

_____

_____

_____

_____

Great-Grandchildren

If you have any great-grandchildren, you may answer any of questions 915 to 928; use your journal or notebook.

Memories of Retirement

Not Yet Retired

945. ☐ Do you plan on retiring? If so, when?

_____

_____

946. ☐ What are your plans? Will you move to another city or country?

_____

_____

_____

_____

947. ☐ Do you look at retirement as "slowing down" or a time of new opportunities?

_____

_____

_____

_____

948. ☐ Do you agree with the mandatory 65 years of age for retirement? Why or why not?

_____

_____

_____

949. ☐ Do you feel that retirement, to some people, means losing one's identity?

_____

_____

_____

_____

Retired

950. ☐ Were you reluctant to retire? If so, why?

_____

_____

_____

_____

_____

951. ☐ Was your retirement sudden or did you have time to plan ahead?

_____

_____

_____

_____

952. ☐ Has retirement been difficult for you and your family? Were there surprises? How have you coped?

_____

_____

_____

_____

_____

953. ☐ What adjustments did you have to make?

_____

_____

_____

_____

_____

954. ☐ Are you concerned about finances? How do you budget your money?

955. ☐ Do you think now that your retirement came too soon? Too late?

956. ☐ Do you still work on a part-time basis? Do you think it is important to keep busy in order to maintain a sense of well-being?

957. ☐ How do you feel about being called a "senior citizen"?

958. ☐ How do you perceive your generation?

_____

_____

_____

_____

959. ☐ Do you feel you have a lot of wisdom to share with people who will listen to you?

_____

_____

_____

_____

_____

960. ☐ Describe a usual day in your life. Do you set goals each day?

_____

_____

_____

_____

961. ☐ What do you do with your leisure time (read, watch television, exercise, travel, watch or participate in sports, do volunteer work, work on a computer)?

_____

_____

_____

_____

_____

962. ☐ Have you been lonely since you retired? If so, what do you do to dispel this mood?

_____

_____

_____

_____

_____

963. ☐ Do you relate to younger people and do you have common interests?

_____

_____

_____

_____

964. ☐ Do you wish that the younger generation were more attentive to the older generation? Why do you believe this does not happen in a lot of families?

_____

_____

_____

_____

965. ☐ Do you socialize with people younger than you or are most of your friends also retired?

_____

_____

_____

_____

966. ☐ Do you spend time with your children and/or grandchildren? If so, how often do you get together?

_____

_____

967. ☐ Would you like more visits from your immediate and extended families? Does it seem as if their lives are very full and that you don't see them as much as you'd like?

_____

_____

_____

_____

968. ☐ Are you concerned about being a burden to your family as you age?

_____

_____

_____

_____

969. ☐ What is it that you fear for your children and/or grandchildren?

_____

_____

_____

_____

970. ☐ Have you experienced any discrimination because of your age? If so, can you relate an example of unfair treatment toward retirees?

_____

_____

_____

_____

971. ☐ Are there certain retirement privileges that you are enjoying?
If so, what are they?

_____

_____

_____

_____

972. ☐ If you are a widow or widower, is being alone difficult? What do
you do for companionship?

_____

_____

_____

_____

_____

973. ☐ Have the things you thought important over the years taken on a
different meaning since retirement? If so, explain what happened.

_____

_____

_____

_____

974. ☐ How would you rate your health at this stage in life? Are there
medical conditions that require you to take medication?

_____

_____

_____

_____

975. ▢   What do you do to keep healthy? Do you believe in taking vitamins? If so, what vitamins do you take on a daily basis?

_____

_____

_____

_____

976. ▢   Do you subscribe to the holistic approach for well-being? Do you watch your fat intake? Are you a garlic eater? Are there certain foods you eat that you are convinced have added extra years to your life?

_____

_____

_____

_____

977. ▢   You may use "home remedies" unique to your family which seem bizarre and funny. Describe them.

_____

_____

_____

_____

978. ▢   How often do you visit a doctor? Are you diligent about getting yearly exams? Do you ever visit a chiropractor?

_____

_____

_____

_____

979. ☐ Does physical exercise play an important part in your daily life? Do you practice yoga? Do you meditate?

980. ☐ Do you consider yourself more energetic or more sedentary than most of your friends?

981. ☐ How would you describe the changes in you, both physically and mentally, over the past few years?

982. ☐ Have you had to curtail certain activities due to poor health? Do you suffer from depression?

983. ☐ If you are not now in a nursing home, would you be prepared at some time to move to one?

984. ☐ What are your feelings about moving into unfamiliar surroundings?

985. ☐ If you are living in a nursing home, what is the best thing about being there? What don't you like?

986. ☐ Looking back, what was the best year of your life? The worst?

987. ☐ Does getting older bother you? Are you glad to have reached the age you are now?

988. ☐ Is the world today moving at too fast a pace for you? What areas concern or confuse you?

_____

_____

_____

_____

_____

989. ☐ Do you think about dying? If you could choose, would you prefer to die at home or in a hospital?

_____

_____

_____

_____

990. ☐ Have you prepared a Living Will? Have you discussed your feelings with members of your family?

_____

_____

_____

_____

991. ☐ Have you signed a donor card for organ transplants in the event you are in an accident or a death occurs? Why or why not? Were you ever a recipient of an organ transplant? If so, what happened?

_____

_____

_____

_____

992. ☐ Have you pre-arranged your funeral? Is your family aware of your wishes? Why do you consider this important?

_____

_____

_____

_____

993. ☐ Has someone close to you died recently? Who was it and how did this death affect you?

_____

_____

_____

_____

994. ☐ Is death easier for you to accept now than it was in earlier years? Describe your feelings.

_____

_____

_____

_____

Thoughts for My Family

995. ☐ What do you appreciate about your family?

_____

_____

_____

_____

_____

996. ☐ What do you wish for them?

_____

_____

_____

_____

_____

997. ☐ What would you caution them about?

_____

_____

_____

_____

_____

998. ☐ Have you any other words of wisdom (or even a poem) that you'd
like to record for future generations?

_____

_____

_____

_____

999. ☐   What would you tell your family your life's lesson has been?

_____

_____

_____

_____

_____

1000. ☐   How do you feel now that you have completed this book as a legacy to your family?

_____

_____

_____

_____

_____

One Final Thought

1001. ☐ If you had to write the last chapter of your life, what would you say?

A Final thought from Patricia A. Williams

Why did I publish this book? For years I have been interested in my past and that of my family. After my father died, I was saddened to realize that he took with him the stories and memories that I did not learn about and record while he was living. It became apparent to me that we need to chronicle our own life experiences and the stories of our parents, grandparents, and other family members before it is too late.

So few of us seem to have the time or take the time for family reminiscing. Many people want to write the stories of their lives but do not know where to begin. By putting the questions about many areas of a person's life into an easy-to-follow book format, I created this "memory tutor" as a key to unlocking those precious recollections.

"Feel what you felt as a child," "journal your past," "nurture your core," "peel back the layers of your life" - advice from people in the helping professions emphasizes how important it is to acknowledge the experiential and spiritual foundations of our lives.

As indicated in the "How to Use this Book" section, *Once Upon a Lifetime...* can help you to record your story at any level that you find appropriate. You may have written a chronological and factual history of your "life and times" for your children and grandchildren. You may have written an intensely personal profile as the beginning of a therapeutic journey into reflection and self-analysis, or as the basis of conversations with the people you care about most deeply. You may not have used the book to tell your own story, but as a resource in transcribing the stories of family members and friends.

Regardless of the role this book has played in your life, I hope you experienced a sense of accomplishment as you used it, and that you came to know yourself or others better as you wrote about past events, present circumstances, and future hopes and expectations in *Once Upon a Lifetime...*

> "When time, which steals our years away,
> Shall steal our pleasures too,
> The memories of the past will stay,
> And half our joys renew."

> – Anonymous –

Mail Order Form - (Book)

(Order Form for computer version on reverse)

Check or money order payable to:

The Time Broker Inc.   Tel: 780-486-3248 Fax: 780-486-2380
P.O. Box 37066   E-mail: pwilliams@storiesofyourlife.com
Edmonton, Alberta   Web: www.storiesofyourlife.com
Canada T5R 5Y2   (order online using VISA or MasterCard)

U.S. orders payable in U.S. funds. Prices subject to change without notice.

$19.95 each book (Cdn.); $14.95 each book (U.S.)
  Shipping: 1-5 books: $7.00

*10% discount for **package of 6 books** ($107.73 Cdn.; $80.73 U.S.)
  Shipping: each pack of 6 books: $7.00

*20% discount for **each case of 48 books** ($766.08 Cdn.; $574.08 U.S.)
  Shipping: each case $22.00   **Large volume discounts offered**

* *Discounts included in above pricing*

No. of units _____   **No. of 6-packs** _____   **No. of cases** _____

TOTAL PRICE FOR BOOKS	$	
Shipping and Handling	$	
SUB-TOTAL	$	
GST/HST Cdn. residents	$	HST (15%) for residents of NF, NB & NS
TOTAL AMOUNT	$	

Name: _____   **Date:** _____

Street: _____

City/Town: _____   **Province/State:** _____

Postal Code/Zip: _____   **Tel:** _____

Fax: _____   **E-mail:** _____

Web: _____

Mail Order Form - *(Computer version)*
(Order Form for book version on reverse)

Check or money order payable to:

The Time Broker Inc.
P.O. Box 37066
Edmonton, Alberta
Canada T5R 5Y2

Tel: 780-486-3248 Fax: 780-486-2380
E-mail: pwilliams@storiesofyourlife.com
Web: www.storiesofyourlife.com
(order online using VISA or MasterCard)

U.S. orders payable in U.S. funds. Prices subject to change without notice.

$19.95 each unit (Cdn.); $14.95 each unit (U.S.)
  Shipping: 1-5 units: $7.00

*10% discount for **package of 6 units** ($107.73 Cdn.; $80.73 U.S.)
  Shipping: each package of 6 units: $7.00

*20% discount for **each case of 48 units** ($766.08 Cdn.; $574.08 U.S.)
  Shipping: each unit $22.00   **Large volume discounts offered**

* *Discounts included in above pricing*

No. of units _____ **No. of 6-packs** _____ **No. of cases** _____

TOTAL COMPUTER VERSION	$
Shipping and Handling	$
SUB-TOTAL	$
GST/HST Cdn. residents	$
TOTAL AMOUNT	$

HST (15%) for residents of NF, NB & NS

Name: _____   **Date:** _____

Street: _____

City/Town: _____   **Province/State:** _____

Postal Code/Zip: _____   **Tel:** _____

Fax: _____   **E-mail:** _____

Web: _____

LOOKING FOR A GIFT?

Once Upon a Lifetime... is an ideal gift for birthdays, Mother's Day, Father's Day, grandparents, Christmas, Hanukkah, anniversaries, retirements, clients, any special occasion – or – just because you care. If you wish gift books to be mailed directly, fill out the gift cards below and include them with your order form. Write the recipients' names and addresses on a separate page.

A Gift of Time

To: _____

_____

From: _____

A Gift of Time

To: _____

_____

From: _____

A Gift of Time

To: _____

_____

From: _____